The Journal

of

John Andrew

Edited by

Harold Lawrence

HERITAGE BOOKS
2024

HERITAGE BOOKS

AN IMPRINT OF HERITAGE BOOKS, INC.

Books, CDs, and more—Worldwide

For our listing of thousands of titles see our website
at
www.HeritageBooks.com

Published 2024 by
HERITAGE BOOKS, INC.
Publishing Division
5810 Ruatan Street
Berwyn Heights, MD 20740

International Standard Book Number
Paperbound: 978-0-7884-3489-1

Table of Contents

Preface

During the year 2000, after having been long interested in the life of John Andrew and in two very old articles appearing in the *Southern Christian Advocate* and the *Wesleyan Christian Advocate* alluding to his journal and containing some fragments from it, correspondence with a descendant bore fruit. Mr. John Andrews of 1700 Lakeview Circle, Gainesville, GA, sent a photocopy of a booklet written by Fred P. Davenport, a school superintendent in Wyandotte, MI. The booklet was entitled, *John Andrew, Patriot*, and contained useful information on the early years of John Andrew taken from the records of Midway Congregational Church, Liberty County, GA, and other sources. Most interesting was a footnote or two in the back of the booklet that identified Miss Nellie Keith of Palmetto, GA, as a descendant who had in her possession (1963), John Andrew's journal, family Bible and letters relating to the Andrew family.

A niece of Miss Keith (2-26-1910 – 1-26-1987), Mrs. Peggy Earnest, of 10350 Hutcheson Ferry Road, Palmetto, GA, had retained a box of Miss Keith's papers. The box contained 4 portions of the journal and a section of poems or hymns written by John Andrew. Mrs. Earnest was gracious enough to loan these materials to me, along with a transcribed separate portion of the journal (the original was not included). These materials constitute the main portion of this volume, supplemented by all other source materials gathered on or about John Andrew. Mrs. Earnest also retained possession of an oil portrait of Mary Overton Cosby Andrew, the wife of John Andrew.

Transcription of the journal was completed during the Christmas holidays of the year 2000, though additional materials extended the project into the next year. A debt of gratitude is owed to Dr. Trap Bowen, then a resident of Milledgeville, who proofed the transcriptions and corrected numerous errors and deciphered many difficult passages. Searches for the remaining portions of the journal and the family Bible are on going.

Harold Lawrence

January, 2001

Introduction

John Andrew was the first Methodist preacher born in the state of Georgia. He was also the father of Bishop James Osgood Andrew, the Southern bishop largely responsible for the division of the Methodist Episcopal Church in 1844 and the establishment of the Methodist Episcopal Church, South. While mentioned in many Methodist histories and in the biography of the bishop, written by George Gilman Smith, Jr., little material has surfaced regarding John Andrew other than scant fragments of his journal which have appeared in the church papers of 1841 and 1908. The originals of these fragments or their fuller texts have not been located.

The four original sections of the journal and the section of Andrew's religious poetry found in this rendering are likely the earliest extant documents of North Georgia Methodism, the first of the journal sections being from the year 1818. Due to Andrew being a school teacher as well as a local preacher, these pages give rare insights into education and ministry in those early times.

Perhaps the most compelling reason that larger portions of Andrew's journal were never published was due to the subject material. Most of the entries revealed an outward struggle with poverty and an inward struggle with sin. Andrew truly wrestled with the angel and was unusually hard on himself, sometimes to the point of self-deprecating failure. These thoughts and feelings would have in no wise inspired or benefited any reader, explaining why only "useful" fragments have ever surfaced in print.

Far from a daily account of people in one's experience or of the events of the day, John Andrew's journal was a spiritual log of his praises and his woes. There is little of genealogical or historical value in his record, but the pages are faithful to an accurate account of the shaping of one's spirit and one's longing to separate from and depart from the influences of the world.

If anything redeemed Andrew's writings, it was his poetry. These simple commentaries upon life in the world and life in the spirit were wonderfully written and, no doubt, compare with the writings of published authors of the period. By far, they are the best products from the pen of John Andrew.

Care was not taken to meticulously describe the errors denoted on some of the transcribed pages or the absences of words from portions of the original that were torn or faded or unclear or unreadable. In most instances, the "drift" of the commentary is not hampered by the failure to recognize a word or two.

In transcribing the journal and poems and placing them with related source material, one gains a rare glimpse of life and conduct in post-Revolutionary Georgia. While Andrew happened to be a minister, he had been a soldier, farmer, property-owner, slave-holder, storekeeper and teacher. Remembered best as the father of a prominent individual, John Andrew's own life and character warrant a full investigation and reflection by those who wish to better understand the early times and those who live through them.

Journal Fragments
1789-1791

The earliest journal entries extant were those supplied to the *Christian Advocate* (12-1-1841) and to the *Southern Christian Advocate* (10-22-1841) by Bishop James O. Andrew. He wrote to the latter paper under the heading, "The Olden Time," the following: "As every thing relating to the earliest movements of Methodism in this country must be interesting to us, I send you a few extracts from the Journal and correspondence of my father, who was among the first itinerant preachers raised up in Georgia. If you judge them worth publication, you can use them." – James O. Andrew, Oxford, GA, 10-8-1841.

Sunday, 3-1-1789   We ride to Ninety-six: large assembly, brother Hull preaches; people very hardened. We ride to Oliver's, and tarry. I exhort.

Monday, 2ⁿᵈ   We ride to Jesse Harrison's. Brother Hull preaches to a large assembly – We tarry.

Tuesday, 3ʳᵈ   Ride to B. Harrows, and brother Hull preaches: —very tender. We join six members. Ride to John Harrow's. Tarry.

Wednesday, 4ᵗʰ   We ride to Posey's. –brother Hull preaches: lively meeting. We part; he goes to friend Grey's, and I tarry at Posey's. Join one.

Thursday, 5ᵗʰ   We ride to Frenchtown. Brother Hull preaches. We have a great shout. I am much blessed. Tarry. I preach at night from Rev. vi 17.

Friday, 6th We set out for Widow Carey's. I go there, brother H. goes to Standard's.

Saturday, 7th We go to Bibb's. Brother H. preaches. Mr. Asbury don't come. We ride to Jones' and dine. We go to night meeting: brother Hull preaches. I exhort –three Baptist preachers exhort. We tarry.

Sunday, 8th We ride to Conference at Merriwether's meeting house: there meet Dr. Coke, Mr. Asbury, and other preachers. Dr. Coke and Mr. Asbury preach to a large assembly. We halt. I tarry at Peter Terrill's.

Monday, 9th Conference begins at Daniel Grant's. The members are, Dr. Coke, President, Francis Asbury, Richard Ivey, Hope Hull, James Conner, Moses Parks, Burge Partridge. Taken on trial, John Andrew, Philip Matthews, John Crawford. Here, indeed, I discover the permanency of the Methodist Church. Bless God that my eyes have seen such a day! Oh the goodness of God that he has directed such a scheme of religion to favour mankind. Monday night we have preaching by brother Partridge; in the day by Coke and Asbury.

Tuesday, 10th Conference breaks about 10 o'clock. Many things determined on very noble. Preachers stationed in Georgia are Conner, Augusta. Harris and Grisson, Richmond. Hull and Massey, Burk. Ivey and Parks, Wilkes. Andrew, Cherokee. Crawford and Mathews sent away.

Dr. Coke and Mr. Asbury preach and ordain Conner and Harris, Deacons; Parks and Hull, Elders. We adjourned.

March 9th, 1790 We ride to meet Bishop Asbury and brother Whatcoat at Sharp's. Brother Whatcoat preaches and we have no stir. We ride to brother Terry's, and dine, then to brother Grant's and tarry –here we stay.

Wednesday, 10th   The Conference opens, and we have a good time, but nothing great – numbers of people – great preaching. Lord help me to improve from it all.

Thursday, 11th   Great congregation. I and those taken on trial with me remain on trial. This night will be long remembered here.

Friday, 12th Conference breaks this day. Great preaching. Brother Hull preaches at night. We have three souls profess. Great work. –tís remarkable, the work!

Saturday, 13th We sat on the business of the College to be erected in this quarter. Preaching moved to chapel Saturday and Sunday. Tarry at Darracoat's.

Sunday, 14th We ride to P.H. Great time indeed: one converted. We now part and I never expect to meet all again in time.

Thursday, March 17, 1791 Ride to Scott's. Meet Dr. Coke and preachers, and open Conference. The preachers present are brother Asbury, brother Coke, brother Ellis, brother Massey, brother Crawford, brother Mathews, brother Holliday, brother Lipsey, brother Holley, brother Harris, brother Grisson.

Friday, 18th We meet; sit all day. Brother Ellis preaches. We sit late and early; much thronged; much fatigued; number of people; great disputes.

Saturday, 19th We attend preaching: both bishops preach. Good times. We retire and sit. Conference breaks. Four preachers ordained; three taken on trial.

Sunday, 20th We have near twelve hundred people. The bishops preach, and we have a work indeed; great cry and they leave us.

It will be perceived from the brief notices of one of the Conferences in the foregoing extracts, that mention is made of the doings of the Conference on the subject of a College to be erected in Georgia; and I have seen in some of our printed books reference to "Wesley College."—These notices go to show that Bishop Asbury, especially at this early day, felt the importance of literary training in connexion with Methodistic influence. But I wish these items published now, in order to elicit information in reference to this said Wesley College. Where was it to have been located? How much was subscribed towards its establishment? and why was it abandoned? – together with any facts connected with the movement towards its establishment. There may be living still, some Methodists of olden time, who may throw some light upon the subject. If so, we wish to hear from them through the columns of the Advocate, as soon as may be. And I take this opportunity to invite the preachers of the Conferences patronizing your paper to employ some pains in collecting such facts and incidents connected with the earlier history and subsequent progress of Methodism in their respective fields of labour, as can be well authenticated, and furnish them for publication. We greatly desire to see a full and authentic history of our beloved Church in the South and Southwest, and we must look to the preachers spread over all the work for the necessary materials. We don't care for fine writing, we want the facts.

**

Journal Fragments
1792

The following fragments from John Andrew's Journal appeared in the *Wesleyan Christian Advocate* on 1-2-1908, supplied to the paper by historian, George Gilman Smith. Smith noted in his article that the journal for the year ended on the 10th of July.

Sunday, 10th June, 1792   This day I went to teach black people and by some means they fail to come and but five attend. We met together and I yet hope God will give me power to prevail with them, conquer their prejudices and persuade them to religion. They have been prejudiced in this neighborhood against the Methodists.

24th   Rose in peace and go to meet the black people, feel comfortable and have a few come and I teach them till 12 o'clock.

George G. Smith recorded another fragment in his volume, *The Life and Times of George Foster Pierce*. 1888, when he wrote of the prejudice against female education. On p. 106, he mentioned the Andrew journal and contributed the following entry from the year 1792:

I was surprised to find Brother Crutchfield averse to his daughters ever learning figures.

Journal
for the year 1818
from the 21st of December
by John Andrew

...(torn)..ember. I begin school ...(torn)...ning. Various mercies have I seen many Comforts have I witnessed but am now in peace. a Day of peace.

31st met quietly, a Day of peace. O for a watchfull Soul, tis a day of importance. the last in the year. What mercies have I known this year, what Trials have I been brought through from Men and things, persecuted by my own brethren. blessed by my Lord and my Salvation.

1st **Day of January 1819,** The Lord has brought me thru **(torn)** the beginning of another Year by Grace I am determined to begin a new life meet in peace.

2nd Stay at home Sleet. and very Cold.

3rd bro. Smith preaches at Prospect very Cold day I am lifeless.

4th Election at Lexington. Day of trial. I am some troubled.

5th Met school in peace a day of Consolation and peace, I am delivered from my fears.

6th Meet in peace. full School, how great provision is made for me, I am this morning troubled with unholy thoughts. They meet for School house mending we are now more Comfortable.

7th Meet in peace, a day of Some Trials but many Blessings.

8th Dark Cloudy day meet quietly this morning part with Betsy Davenport moves to Franklin Tender time.

9th labour at home bro. Smith stays with me at home this night a most agreeable time.

10th ride to Madison to a meeting good time hardened people. return very Sick indeed … a night of pain. Lord give me more life and power.

11th Meet in peace and quiet a day of peace and quiet.

12th Cloudy dark morning and a more Cloudy mind, meet in peace and quiet, my reflections during the night have been solemn. O for thoughts of God more deeply.

13th Meet in peace: great are my trials. Great also are my Comforts. O for grace.

14th Meet safely. Can I doubt the mercies of God. I am deeply affected with the case of Spencer my Son-in-law. He is a man of an excellent Spirit in many things, but he by a habit of horse Swapping, has ruined himself and family, and has finally left them, without provision, and been gone since the 10th inst: I am not able to provide for them, I have a wife and 6 children dependant on my exertions. he has left a wife and 4 children.

I am now sixty years of age and no one to help me: Corn is from one to two dollars per bushell, pork from 8 to 10 Dollars per hundred, what must I do. I have only to do all I can and trust to providence. He has never forsaken me.

15th meet in peace. a Day of quiet. too much I fear.

11

16th   This morning I am Surprized by George Spencer   What am I to do   I must relieve him. we are On to N. Merriwethers for corn   late before we get home. time of trial.

17th   We go to meeting. at prospect.   good Sermon.   but alas how dull.

18th   Meet in quiet. tis a day of some trial   yet many Trials.

19th   Meet safely   Cloudy mor.g *(morning)*   I am not well. a Day of peace.

20th   This evening recieve a letter from my Son   he Sends me ten dollars. what a Son.   his Station is in Columbia SC.

21st   meet in peace and quiet. live in peace   enjoy peace with my God.   and in my dear family. Yet am I too lifeless. I love too little.

22nd   tis a publick Day. no School meet at Brightwells. O How I feel for poor deluded Souls. They gather to Drink and Sin. I am not as I wish. too Stupid and lifeless.

23rd   Stay and labour hard at home. a Day of Great trial and pain.

24th   I am now in Solitude. Sabbath morning, O when Shall I Serve God as I ought to do. Lord give me a happy morning. I am to go for: Prospect. I did so and Pope preached *(I've)* felt well but I am too dull.

25th   I am met in peace — tis a day of quiet a fine School. O may I live more holy.

26th   I have met in quiet tis a great mercy of God I have a school for next year am provided for abundantly a morng of temptation. yet I have power to Conquer. the Day passes in peace.

27th Meet in peace and quiet and have a Day of Quiet. one day more of mercies proves the long forebearance of God toward a dying world: and to me.

28th This morning is peace. I would here remark. I never knew a Year of so little rain. This winter. Scarce any and January appears like May. the day passes in external peace.

29th Meet Safely. very Dry no rain the day passes quietly.

30th Stay at home. go to prospect *(Circt. for circuit)* Preacher comes. Green. We have a good meeting. Blessed be god he has sent us preachers this year.

31st Sabbath. I am here in silence and I hope with God. tis Class meeting day. I go to meet the people. but five meet. Lord look on Zion in this place and revive thy work.

Notes: 3rd & 9th The minister on the Appalachee Circuit in 1818 was Thomas A. Smith who was on the Broad River Circuit in 1819 and who located by 1822. It is possible that this was the preacher to whom Andrew was referring in his entries, though in February & March, he named James Smith as the preacher. **8th** Franklin was an early name for Athens, GA, though it is more likely that Andrew referred to the county of Franklin rather than to Athens. **20th** The son referred to was James Osgood Andrew (1794-1871), later bishop, who served Columbia in 1819. **24th** The Pope who preached is unknown. He was too early to be Benjamin Blanton Pope (1804 – 1835) who entered the conference in 1828. Benjamin was the son of Henry Pope. Henry A. Pope and his brother Burrell Pope were responsible for the entity called Pope's Chapel in the Wolfskin District of Oglethorpe County and an earlier one by that name in Wilkes. **30th** The preacher who came was likely Raleigh

13

Green (1797-1857) who probably located in that area in 1821. He was on the Oakmulgee Circuit in 1818, the Little River Circuit in 1819, and the Appalachee Circuit in 1820.

1st   **Day of February**: frost. we have had fine rain. meet in peace and quiet. I have a large School on Saturday I enjoyed much, on Sabbath I had Violent temptation. God gave me Victory.

2nd   Cold and frosty. Meet in peace last night I felt as I hardly ever do my Dreams on my bed have troubled me much nor Can I know their meaning.

3rd   I have met in peace rainy Day. I am now in hope. O for a clean heart. I long to be entirely given up to God.

4th   Met in peace: tis a day of trial yet of Great mercy to me.

5th   When just ready to start for School Lr. (**unk.**) Johnson comes and I have to go for Petersburg in Elbert. I find he when in liquor has been guilty of a shameful matter we stay at Mat. Williams who is very kind to us. (Note: the word Mat. is followed with a w).

6th   We ride to Petersburg. find the business dolefull. he when drunk overset his wagon burst a box of goods and lost many. we settle all matters. and find he will have to pay at least 150 Dollars in all. rains on us to Williams. are kindly received, and well treated. I am taken with a bad cold and fever. am very sick.

7th   Sabbath. I am obliged to travel in the rain home very sick and very wett, sick all night. I never hardly knew such a night. rain wind thunder lightning yet.

8th   This day meet safely in School yet sick but few scholars. Rainy Day passes in peace.

9th I am at Lr. Johnsons what will not drunkenness do he in a drunken frolick has beat Ed. martin. in another fought Jb. Eberheart and then oversett his waggon as above said. then abused Roseberry and Subjected himself to a lawsuit. Meet in peace. Still rainy.

10th Meet in peace. I am low in the Spirit Turns Cold Close the Day in peace.

11th Meet in peace Cold Morning but becomes warm, and Clouds up day passes in peace.

12th Meet in peace so dark I Can Scarcely see. This has been an uncommon phoenomenon Some planet must have passed the face of the sun for about half an hour. it became as twilight I could neither read nor write the Scholars laid down their books. afterward very rainy till near night.

13th Stay at home and find peace of Soul Go to meeting bro. Ogletree preaches I am too Dull Cold day Society dull. good Preacher.

14th I am here this Sabbath morning in Silence. O may it be a day of Joy and happiness to all God's people. Class meeting Day. I go and return good meeting. enjoyed a Calm evening. but no ecstasy.

15th Meet in great peace. Cold morning. This morning Betsy comes & Lucy. blessed be god for all his mercies.

16th Safely meet. but O how lifeless rains, and I am not satisfied with myself. O for life.

17th Meet in peace, wet Day. go home in quiet.

18th   Meet in peace Betsy goes for franklin to day and we are troubled.

19th   Meet Safely very Cold day various are my trials yet no great event.

20th   I am at home very unwell, no great matter, Day passes in peace, yet I do lament my unfaithfulness.

21st   Sabbath Day I am here in Solitude O may I but meet my Master. Preaching today at Prospect I go, hoping to meet the Lord. Adieu ye groves for a while, where I have often felt a silent Joy in solitude. I have been to meeting but alas how little do I feel   return home but lament that I feel so little.

22nd   Meet in quietness. tis a Day of some trial but many favours O for more religion. Lord revive my Soul.

23rd   Meet in peace. Cloudy Day My Soul is heavy and Sick. tired of every thing and every person Lord Set me right.

24th   Cloudy Day meet in peace day passes in quiet.

25th   Meet quiet Dark morning. Trials await me. but I am in the hands of God let him do his good pleasure.

26th   Meet in peace and quiet. a day of peace.

27th   a Day of labour and pain meeting Day go Jas. Smith Preaches. Great Sermon, but I have no feeling.

28th   Sabbath Day, I am here and in Silence but no joy meeting Day but few, & cold.

Notes: 13th The preacher on that occasion was probably Philemon Ogletree who was on the Grove Circuit in 1818 and the Little River Circuit in 1819.

1st **March.** Meet in peace tis a morning of trial. a day of trouble, but I am in the hands of God. Can any thing happen to hurt me. O no I have the Divine promises I must, I will trust him.

2nd Meet this morning in peace O what a world this is what Contention Lord Deliver me from all men.

3rd We are met in peace, tis a Day of quiet. day closes in peace.

4th Meet Safely Tis a Day of Some Trial yet peace & health.

5th Stay at home. go labour.

6th labour at home a Day of some trial much fatigue.

7th Sabbath Day, I am here, what Silence reigns in this Shade, not a whisper, not a foot fall, even the birds are Silent, only a humming bee is heard from the wood. The voice of God alone I hear reproving me for my unholiness and unfaithfulness. O for Zeal in thy Sacred Cause. Tis James Smith preaches today a man I love, yet I know tis vain if God is not present. I'll go.

8th Meet in peace and quiet yesterday. I went and heard two excellent Sermons from Jas. Smith & Christian Yet O how Stupid: I felt when shall I be as I wish to be. Lord help me to overcome.

9th I am here in peace. O that this day may be better than the last.

10th Go to town various are my feelings neglected by some: slighted by others persecuted by many. See many Indians View them with wonder at the wonders of Gods works.

11th Meet Safely dark day and wett This Day passes in peace.

12th I am here this morning in peace, a day of some trial but it passes in peace and quiet.

13th at home meeting Day at prospect bro. Ogletree preaches. no stirr. tis proposed to Society relative to my preaching. and they Consent to it. I hope I have not erred in this matter. I would not enjure that Sacred Cause.

14th Sabbath Day. I am lifeless. I find too much desire to be respected. James Smith preaches his farewell sermon great indeed. This day *(Mrs.)* Bradley dies.

15th Meet School in peace the Day passes in outward peace yet the day is dark Cloudy and perhaps the darkest evening two hours before sunset.

16th meet in peace & quiet. This day is very blustering and cold yet have I peace and quiet.

17th meet in quiet a very Cold morning and very hard frost and ice. fruit I expect all killed.

18th This morning is dark and cloudy meet in peace but alas how many days pass and still I am dull and lifeless. alas shall I ever be as I wish on this side of the grave. No. I never expect it. I see now the policy of the enemy. to keep me involved that I may never be in quiet of mind. I have much to Struggle with, yet god has given me much mercy, Shall I then doubt of his love, his goodness. no. I will trust him though he Slay me.

19th I have met in peace and quiet. Yet my Dreams last night were uneasy and painful. I am old, and have more to do than my strength will bear.

20th Day of labour at home time of trial indeed.

21st Sabbath. Sett out for Wm. D **(unk.)** in Franklin County much against my will, for I condemn riding on the Sabbath day. meet various trials on the road arrive about five, find them well. 35 miles.

22nd Stay in franklin, various trifling scenes. take place. I don't like this county.

23rd This day meant to start homeward but rains incessantly, till about nine at night. O what pains of mind I feel from being absent this evening *(Mr.)* Shannon Comes over, and begins a dispute on religion, I find him insensible of the first principles of it am enabled to Combat his opinion.

24th Start this morning for home dark and cloudy, Patsy behind me we have a pleasant Day we are blessed, great time of trial get home safe, find all well.

25th meet school once more in peace Tis a day of quiet and peace.

26th meet quietly a day of peace.

27th first day of quarterly meeting many preachers, good Sermons, few people good Day to me, I am licensed to exhort. O may I be faithfull Lord help me to be more Devoted.

28th This Day is a great Day to one and to many Souls. good meeting I hope it will be the beginning of a revivall to many Souls. I am here in Silence the world shut out. I have strong confidence. this Day I am started anew my wife for the first time spoke in love feast O how I am blest.

29th Meet in peace and quiet. tis a Day of peace, this night is rainy thunders and lightens. find myself still I am bound for heaven.

30th all is peace and Safety. Cloudy and dark very windy. tis a day of peace but alas I am so soon interrupted by worldly things.

31st We are met in peace, and have a Day of great peace, yet I have some trials, O for victory over my besetting Sins. I have felt them this evening.

Notes: 8th Gabriel Christian had located from the traveling ministry in 1807 and made his home in Oglethorpe County. In 1819, he was a trustee at Prospect Meetinghouse where John Andrew attended and likely had continued as a local preacher.

1st **April.** This morning I see ice. and O, I am pursued for money and can't pay it. I must fly to my only refuge for help. I suppose I was wrong to contract those debts, but what could I do, my family was large, I had no money I bought I think only what was needfull, and we live very hard, my School would not furnish meat and bread, to beg I was ashamed, what could I do, I thought another year would enable me to pay all. Lord forgive if I have erred.

2nd Meet a few Scholars, cold and cloudy. I have a peace that not all this world can give, yet I cannot rest till I feel more and can get clear of the world.

3rd   Labour at home, feel too much, of wrong tempers rains I am wet end the day uncomfortably.

4th   Sabbath. go to bradly's. bro. Hodges preaches funerall, many People good Sermon. return home and go to L. Johnsons, he is sick and I fear not prepared to die.

5th   Meet the School in peace but alas has nature yet not been Conquered. This day I have been more encouraged than common to persevere in religious ways. O for more life.

6th   Met Safely. and feel a firm hope a day of quiet and peace, great is divine goodness to a worm of dust.

7th   Safely met very few scholars. Cold and frost great prospect of Wheat now, Day Closes in peace, fine weather.

8th   This morning I am in peace and quiet fine morning pleasant Day. it passes in peace and health.

9th   fine Spring morning: very few scholars have peace and quiet. this week I have had more real enjoyment than usual.

10th   labour at home tis a morning of great peace yet am I much tired by night, and suffer much, yet would I prefer a life of labour to any other, but the will of providence be done. Lord give me patience.

11th   Sabbath. I go in pain to Class, but now O Lord revive thy work among us Company Comes in I am disordered, spend the Day too much in vain Conversation.

12th   labour at home tis easter Day a day of pain indeed. very sore my wife Starts to Elbert after being four years absent from it.

13th meet School in peace –the day passes in quiet and no material Circumstance happens.

14th by mercy we are again met in peace. nothing important happens this Day. in evening God blessed me much.

15th Rainy. Yet fruit enough left we are met in peace and quiet, how often have I written thus, Yet the day will come, when I must write it no more. Close the Day in peace.

16th Met in peace no thing great occurs Day passes in quiet.

17th Labour at home. various are the scenes of this day to me yet God blesses me I am in health, my children in health. I have bread and enjoy religious society Glory to God.

18th Sabbath of my Lord I wish to be this day devoted more than ever to my God. I have left my family and retired here, in hopes of meeting him whom my soul loveth, I think I shall not be disappointed. I was not disappointed tis a precious morning to me and I am happy, go to meeting bro. A. Smith preaches. I am not pleased with the Sermon. I fear too much party Spirit reigns and I tremble for Zion.

19th Meet in peace, my wife returns last night. O what a day have I had blessed be my Lord O may I never loose thy favour.

20th Meet in peace and quiet. tis a day of peace and quiet yet not as happy as some days past. I close the Day in peace.

21st Tis a Day of quiet and peace.

22nd Meet in quiet – pass the Day in peace and find but few trials God is mine.

23rd Meet quietly Cloudy I am very unwell in body the day passes in quiet.

24th Day of labour at home, much fatigued.

25th Sabbath. no appointment for meeting. I am here in quiet Solitude. nothing interrputs my peace How Sweet the moments of retirement to me, I love my Lord, yet how Cold. lord give me strength to rise. I am here in the evening, yet how dark. alas the Cause is in me the Cause is in me though I now see it not. Lord thou knowest my feeble frame, I am determined to be at his feet and implore his mercy. heavy rain and thunder.

26th Meet in Safety, but far from peace. this is a day of trial to me. I am Surrounded, involved, and know not how to escape, Old and infirm, yet a numerous family to support, provisions high. Lord, help Can only Come from thee. O hide not thy face.

27th *A day* rainy we meet only three rainy wett I am very unwell in body and soul.

28th I am here in peace and have a day of quiet yet am I not in peace till night. in family prayer, my Soul is tendered. O how precious is one glance of Gods presence, ten thousand worlds should not buy one moments enjoyment from me. O could I live as I wish I would never wander from my God for a moment.

29th meet in peace. Cloudy for three days past yea five, and much rain, the day passes quietly, but I feel not as I wish. my Soul enjoys not the peace I wish.

30th I am met in peace yet Cloudy and my Soul is yet Dark and heavy, but I must *(endure)* in hope and in Confidence, my Lord will yet Come. And I will wait on him.

Notes: 4th bro. Hodges was likely Samuel K. Hodges (d. 1840) who was on the Little River Circuit in 1813 and was the Presiding Elder of the area from 1818-21. **18th** A. Smith may have been Rev. Anderson Smith (1788-1884), father of Rev. Seaborn Smith, or Rev. Anthony G. Smith (1776-1852) but there are no service records on either.

*

Here this section of the journal ends on the last inside page of the section. On the back page, however, there is more writing that appears to be a fragment of another day of another month. It is torn and frayed, being an outside page. What is written appears as follows:

21st Monday. Meet in peace. I must now record the goodness of the Lord. On Saturday night I was lamenting my want of money, to get a little meat for we had none. I dreamed some one paid me money: next day I received a letter containing 4 **(torn)** Dollars. O divine goodness.

Rainy day no Scholars. Stay awhile and have much retirement than go home. Have break up til new year. I expect many Sorrows but if God be for me who will be against me. go to mill. I **(torn:** the last word of this line is faded, the next two lines are torn away with the last word of the last line being, "school.").

***

Second Section

While this section picks up on May 1st, it is not known if it is the same year as the above due to the fact that the pages are of a different size, appearing not to have come from the same book. The mention of bro. Pope, a preacher on the Appalachee Circuit in 1828-29 would likely place this section in those years, but the 4th section was from 1828 and the 5th transcribed section (the original not having been available) was from 1829, crossing some of the same months. The pages physically correspond with those of section 4, which place them at the later period.

Due to the correspondence of dates historically with correct calendar years, the only possibilities for this section are 1824 and 1830. Since Andrew died in 1830, it is probable that this section was written in 1824.

1st May being Saturday: I am at home, my wife starts for Franklin: I am taken very sick tis a day of pain, I sorrow: rains hard Stormy night:

2nd   Sabbath Day no preaching tis a Solemn day to me at home, but alas how little do I feel. Why O why am I thus I know the fault is mine, O when shall I be delivered. let me wait the will of God.

3rd   Meet safely this morning, a day of quiet I am pained at my own supineness, fair Day.

4th   Meet in quiet. Cloudy no rain this day is peace and quiet.

5th   I am safely met good weather I am still in deadness. This day I feel greater confidence than usual. Death is nigher, I am led to try my evidence and blessed be God I feel that I am his.

6th   We are met in peace, tis a fine morning, I have a lively hope. but I have not that life in my Soul I wish to have. Yet will I wait in patience and hope, I feel that I shall be yet delivered.

7th   Met in peace and quiet. Lord help me to live better. nothing material happens during the day.

8th   a Day of labour yet blessing. fine weather, great prospect of a plentiful crop of all kinds of grain.

9th   Sabbath Day. Class meeting few people, promising young man for a leader. I exhort for the first time since admitted and we had a good time. This evening The Lord blesses me in a Singular manner.

10th   meet in health and quiet: dark Cloudy morning: much thunder some hail little rain fair evening ride meet my wife, bring her home.

11th   Meet in peace and quiet, a fine day, no material Circumstance happens.

12th   all is well nothing happens very material during the day O if I could but be resigned to my lott.

13th   Meet in peace it has been a day of peace of Joy, of love to me, I thank my God for religion, for Charity, for a feeling (13th continued), O could I even feel thus I should not envy a King but alas you change O ye Scenes of Sorrow why will ye come.

14th   Meet in peace, yet my Soul is too lifeless my body is Sick. very sick. tis therefore a day of Sorrow.

15th Day of labour at home rains a day of trial and trouble.

16th This is the Lords day and I am here in peace and quiet O may my Lord meet me here and make it a Day of Joy, I would live holy, but so it is my way is hedged up, This world lies in my way. not that I love it, but I long to have enough to pay what I owe and to support my family: but I am a poor Creature Sometimes I fear I shall never get Safe. Tis meeting Day, I go Lord meet us. I went we had a good sermon no stirr.

17th meet in peace. cold and windy Day, to my soul tis Cold and Stormy. Yet I hope.

18th tis a day of Storm O how I hate myelf. for these dolefull feelings I endure with the Hypocondriac Oh what I would do for my relief meet in peace Day of peace.

19th Cold yet Cloudy. meet Safely This day at evening I am much blessed. Closes in peace.

20th Meet Safely tis a day of quiet rains a little.

21st Meeting day, I go, bro. Green preaches, I am greatly blessed indeed good day to many, Day ends in great peace and quiet.

22nd Day of labour at home, I am unwell, yet labor hard. I find it hard to get provisions can I do more, let me not repine but be thankfull. God is mine.

23rd I am here, yet how sleepy, dull inactive and stupid, Lord deliver me from all Sin, I go to meeting no I did not go. I am sick and tempted, but I stay at home am dull lifeless sick, fear I have done wrong.

24th   Meet in peace   I am yet lifeless   fine rain this evening indeed   Called off to Settle some buisness with Pittman and Johnson N. Merriwether and wife   have staid all night.

25th   Meet in peace tis a fine day the day passes in peace and quiet O could I recall my past life how soon would I forget the scenes of rebellion.

26th   Meet in quiet this morning. fine morning yet it rains at night good rain thunders hard. O my Soul why so lifeless.

27th   Cloudy, meet in peace day passes quietly and no trouble rain at night O I feel much darkness and doubting.

28th   Meet in quiet. the boys have shut me out but I get in and consent to break up early.

29th   Day of labour   pain and trial   I labour hard   am indeed sick. Carry my wife at night to bro. Christians. She is unwell.

30th   Sabbath go to old bro. Andrews to funeral: bro. Christian & bro. Jones speak. good time, return take my wife home. She is very Ill all night.

31st   Whitsuntide. holy day   at home. labour hard   am much *worked.*

1st   **June.** Meet in peace   a day of some trial, yet some peace O could I gain Confidence.

2nd   Meet safely and happily   this Day passes in quiet   the night in peace but O my Soul. what Sorrows have I seen.

3rd   Meet quietly yet I am not alive to God. O I am not as *I* wish to be the day passes.

4 Tis Friday and, we are met in peace O for more faith. a day of quiet.

5 Day of labour at home and a day of great trial. yet it passes in great peace and quiet. I am now destitute of meat and can get none Yet must I submit.

6 Tis a Sabbath day my soul is Calm yet not lively yet I pass the day in quiet.

7 Meet in peace tis a day of peace but alas I cannot, I do not feel as I wish, if I have religion how little life and power, I will try to hold my Saviour with a trembling hand Lord give me life from **(unfinished)**.

8 I am met quietly but not in peace of Soul as I wish. The day passes in peace. O for a Closer walk with God.

9 This morning I am met in great peace, I felt in private a firm Confidence. O how dark.

10 I have met in quiet, but not in peace my Soul is in heaviness, this day I have taken cold and am very unwell, my cow calves, and tis dead a loss indeed to us, we have been near six months without milk yet I feel resigned, tis somehow for the best. Gods will be done.

11 Meet in peace, Cloudy rain much wanting tis a day of trial.

12 day for labour. I am at home, go to merriwethers, for corn, rains get wett. am very unwell.

29

13th   Sabbath day. I am here, yet am sick, tis Cloudy. I have peace but not as I wish. O my Soul examine and see why these sorrows, thou hast been too unfaithfull indeed.

14th   Yesterday I was sick. I staid at home and alas I feel condemned   I hear they had a good meeting   Meet in quiet this morning. had a fine rain. I will trust of my lord.

15th   Meet Safely cool pleasant morning   I feel more confidence O for meekness   I long to conquer every passion and every sinfull temper.

16th   I am met in peace and quiet   Cloudy morning   last night I was blessed in private prayer. O how sweet   Day passes in quiet.

17th   Cloudy morning   no rain. I felt last night some comfort day is peace and quiet.

18th   I am now at home and tis meeting Day. good Sermon   few people, taking in of Mrs. black   Comes on, causes much debate. She is at last received.

19th   day of labour at home, good rain   day Closes in peace and quiet.

20th   Sabbath day   bro. Smith preaches. a great sermon   for the first time in many years I am called on to exhort publickly, O how I feel   the day Closes in quiet.

21st   Meet School in peace, a day of quiet and peace.

22nd   Meet quietly indeed   fine Day.   no rain   much wanting. Day Closes in peace.

23ʳᵈ   Meet in peace, fine day. I am however too lifeless.

24ᵗʰ   I am now here in great peace   Cloudy day   no rain, this evening is a good rain.

25ᵗʰ   Today we meet in peace. Tis cool and fair. alas how little I feel of religion   I long to be made entirely holy.   Lord help me.

26ᵗʰ   labour at home   tis a day of pain   tired and troubled.

27ᵗʰ   Sabbath day   Bro. Pope preaches   a good meeting I feel but alas how little.   I am here but don't feel that flow I will still long for.

28ᵗʰ   Meet in peace and quiet   very dry weather   I never knew a better harvest year   no rain to injure fine Crops of wheat, promising Crops of Corn and Cotton, tis a very remarkable year for honey and bees   much honey *dew.*

29ᵗʰ   Meet in peace   no rain. very windy and we suffer for want of rain.

30ᵗʰ   Meet safely   no rain. about 12 it Clouds up and we have very hard hard **(prob. meant hail).**

Notes: 27ᵗʰ Bro. Pope is probably Benjamin Blanton Pope (1804-1835) who was on the Appalachee Circuit in 1828-29.

1ˢᵗ   **July.** Meet Safely –a cool pleasant Day, I find this Spring has been very memorable for much hail and very large, many Crops have suffered much by it. Crops are fine.

2ⁿᵈ   Meet in peace and quiet: very Cool. I am in hope   a day of quiet.

3ʳᵈ   labour at home a day of trial from my besetting sin of unclean and unholy affections.

4ᵗʰ   Sabbath Day. Christian preaches. I go but alas how sleepy dull and inactive am I become. (continued). I am now retired but how little do I feell of religion. I went to meeting, great sermon no stirr O how I felt the power of unbelief get a letter from my son, find he has been very sick.

5ᵗʰ   meet in peace tis a day of peace to us Cloudy but no rain. we are in health.

6ᵗʰ   meet Safely Cloudy, O I am still lifeless but have hope a day of peace and quiet to us.

7ᵗʰ   Meet in quiet. no rain cloudy   a day of peace.

8ᵗʰ   meet in peace rainy morn.g: indeed what a blessing, fine Crops of every kind.

9ᵗʰ   I am now here in peace fine rain we have had still Cloudy Day passes in peace.

10ᵗʰ   tis a day for labour at home am unwell and have much pain.

11ᵗʰ   Sabbath morning am here but alas, how lifeless and dull. in pain of body. Class meeting day. I have been after a severe struggle and returned good meeting.

12ᵗʰ   Meet in peace. tis a day of peace I have hope.

13ᵗʰ   Meet Safely. day passes in quit. *quiet.* Tis a day of victory to my Soul.

14th Meet in peace yet is it a day of some trial, but I feel some Confidence in God.

15th Meet in quiet this morning O for more faith a day of trial indeed with *(Mrs)* Roseberry but I feel conscious of my innocence.

16th Meet under vast trialls. tis meeting day. I cant go. tis a day of trial.

17th day of labour **(unk.)** riding at home.

18th Sabbath, no meeting. today a day of trial indeed O when shall I keep as ought the Sabbath Day.

19th meet in quiet. fine rain Cool day day of peace and quiet.

20th fine morning, meet in peace no interruption to us yet boys improve.

21st we are met in peace tis a fine day. I have confidence tis a Day of Trial yet am I safe.

22nd fine morning meet in peace Day of trial I am overcome by Anger, Lord help me to watch.

23rd Meet in peace. nothing material Occurs this Day.

24th Day of labour at home rains I am blessed.

25th Sabbath Day Class meeting. I am here in Solitude find my Confidence Strong I have been much blessed. I go. I did not go. I am blessed with my Polly Coming with her Children. my betsy Comes in the evening.

26th   Meet in peace this morning   tis a day of rain.

27th   rainy morning indeed   meet in quiet   large School. Day does pass is in peace and quiet this morning my Soul is blest.

28th   Meet Safely. rainy a day of some trial. passes in quiet.

29th   This is a spare day at home. a day of trial and disappointment.

30th   Meet Safely. tis a day of hurry

31st   at home Perplexed disturbed harrassed tormented. yet blest greatly.

1st   **August.** Sabbath: brother Christian preaches at Prospect. Dull time and I am not right: I am here this evening, dull, Sleepy, and lifeless.

2nd   Meet in quiet … and have a day of peace   no rain.

3rd   Come in peace   fine morng this morning I have more light, more Confidence glory to God forever in the evening I am sent for to L. Johnsons   he is very Ill: yet he is spared.

4th   Meet in peace, fine Morning day of hurry.

5th   Meet safely a day of preparation for the exhibition.

6th   This is the day of our exhibition. Meet early we have sixty different appearances on the Stage, the boys perform to admiration and are applauded by all, who have any judgement in matters. Day ends in peace.

7th   labour at home. a day of some trial yet peace.

8th   Sabbath day. Class today. I go. O for a great day. I did go, and such a day I have not lately seen at prospect. happy time of Joy love and peace.

9th   Met in peace. Tis a day of Confusion, recovering from the relaxation of the exhibition.

10th   rainy morning. how blest have we been this year we have not suffered for rain. fine fruit plenty too. great Crops of wheat fine prospect of Corn and *(Cotton)* peace and plenty, what nation is like unto us. O that men would praise the Lord. met in peace.

11th   Last evening, in the Close, I was uncommonly moved to exhort my Scholars, I was set at liberty, spoke some time my soul felt some wept. all were Solemn: Lord water the seed. meet in peace.

12th   This is a wett morning, we are met in quiet. I feel a greater deadness to the world. O for a Clean heart.

13th   meet Safely. dark morning rainy. I am this morning beset with an old temptation. Lord deliver me from every sin from this day.

14th   I am now at home labor hard, very hot day a day of trial. O for a day of peace.

15th   This is a day of Joy a day of Devotion go to Class, great meeting. O what deadness.

16th   Meet in peace wet Day have this night great rain, and my Soul is much blessed. yet soon I have heavy trials.

17th Cloudy morning. for three nights I have had dreams to me I fear Ominous. Some heavy trials I fear are before me. but I cannot fear I am the Lords, and nothing can hurt me but by thy permission.

18th I am relieved glory to God. I have last night the most deep and solemn reflections of God and his power in the midst of a most tremenduous thunder storm I ever saw O how powerfull that God we have to do with –continues- *(page break)* very with *(with marked through)* Cloudy dark and wett Cloudy indeed met in peace- - -

19th we are met in peace and quiet Cloudy day indeed and rains. about two weeks we have had rain and thunder. I have some Confidence.

20th Settled rain, meet a few I have last night had some temptation. O for more faith and love.

21st labour at home very hot day it rains very hard, some trials.

22nd I am in many trials. go to the meeting bro Pope preaches good day to many. rains. great trials Lord undertake for me. or I fall. but shall I doubt the Lord has never forsaken me. O man man. how unfeeling.

23rd Meet in quiet. a few very rainy a day of trouble pain and sorrow.

24th Meet in peace I think after near four weeks wett we shall have fair weather, O how I feel harrassed surrounded.

25th I am relieved last night believe I love God. feel yet determined meet in peace rains yesterday no rain rains all day.

26th fine morning. meet in peace few scholars. live in dread O to be delivered from all men.

27th tis meeting Day, we have no Preacher he did not come, we go home full of disappointment deadness and fear.

28th labour at home in great weakness of body a time of Trial.

29th tis Sabbath I am here. in Solitude but the Cares, and Sorrows of the world Surround me, yet I have hope. tis preaching day and I go. farewell ye Scenes of Solitude till I return.

30th I went yesterday to meeting, we had a very great meeting, at night to hear young Lacy a babtist Preacher: I feel much in the Day. we meet this morning in peace. Cloudy day. rains some.

31st Yesterday concluded in peace and this begins in quiet. Yet my Soul is not in peace, I have been imprudent. I have involved myself in debt. my family when I came here were in want. I had not money. I could not bear to see them suffer, knowing I had been the cause of many sorrows. I expected to be able from my school to pay all, but alas my school, from the very high price of provisions, though we have lived in poverty, will Scarcely Support us. and I am troubled at the thought. that I shall not be able to pay what I owe. alas, am I Cast into the world to be a continual stumbling block to others. Nay, but my own imprudence Continually does it; well I will go like the Prodigal, I will confess my faults, and trust my precious God who has so often delivered me. Lord thou knowest.

***

Third Section

This section is called third simply because it is the third one to be entered. If the second section is a continuation of the first (and that is not known because it is undated) this one is of a different year because it begins in the last days of July of a particular year. Both it and the first section are the most heavily damaged, yet the tone and subject material vary little. As to its date, it could only have been in the year **1817** or **1823**. Probably it is dated **1817**. This section mentions a bro. Harris preaching. The only Harris of record assigned to the Little River Circuit in those years was West Harris who served it in 1815. Harris served Appalachee Circuit in 1816 and located in 1817, probably in the general area.

24th   no meeting last night   very wet. I have a painfull night and this is so wett I don't go to School O what I Suffer. yet how am I blest with patience in this I hope I have   I have been made to conquer, fretfullness has even been my besetting Sin; I find comfort in reading the life of Rev. John Elliot the scripture given me this morg. *(morning)* is: I will be thou *Clean (?):*

25th   This morning I am here some thing better yet in pain still. Cloudy. we have had much rain *(torn)(today)* and it is a *(torn).*

26th   This morning at day light I was attacked in a very severe ma *(torn) (manner)* with the most Severe pain; and must have died soon if I had not been relieved in the evening I was relieved but I canot tell what I suffered.

27th Sabbath day; I am yet in pain thro this day, my Sufferings are great but my Soul is Stayed on god, I have delight in reading and meditation I cried to the Lord in my affliction and he heard me.

28th rains and I am Still in pain. thro this day medicine has no effect. nothing Can relieve till God Shall Speak the word. O *(torn)* *(what)* is man how feeble. how *(torn)*.

29th This morning I thought I would arise and go to School, but alas I was Suddenly seized, and brot. *(brought)* low, and if if the lord had not Stopt the fleeting breath it must have fled but Suddenly, the medicine which had refused to operate, now: when he who had holden me a prisoner for five days Spake the word; obeyed the divine command and, I was delivered; when a few more hours of Such pain, must have Closed the Scene. I was Soon relieved and now enabled to praise God for heath *(health)* returned. by night only a Soreness remained of all my pain: and I Slept in peace after waking for the most of five nights.

30th This morning I am weak but easy and now my Soul, know, that god has intended this Sickness, to let thee learn some important lesson. Search then and know it: and loose not the Visitation. I find I have had too high an opinion of my attainments, as if they were not given I must be more humble. again I find, I have long been too fretfull and have not been patient as I ought, I will beg for Victory over it. I find I have been remarkably kept in all my Sickness. O Lord I Thank thee for all thy mercies and help me to learn more and more. I am now very weak, and long to go to prayer meeting but must not. none meet scarcely.

31st Once more by divine goodness I am here, and O what reason to praise god for all his goodness to me. I have this day had peace and have Seen the Salvation of God to the people, and to me of late.

1ˢᵗ   **Day of August.** This Day I am home but don't feel in Soul as I wish to do tis friday.

2ⁿᵈ   labour at home   a day of heat and fatigue. Yet I have strength but O I am ungaurded *(unguarded)* and am overcome by frettfullness. This day I See the need of more watchfulness. and by Grace I am bound to fight so long as I live. Lord help me to pray and fight.

3ʳᵈ   Sabbath. I Strive to begin this day aright tis meeting day and I go   bro. Harris preaches dull time   return home   find some relief, day closes in peace.

4ᵗʰ   I am here, and feel bound for heaven.   fine morning   I have many Scholars. much trouble this evening. I feel a nearness to God. Lord draw me to thee.

5ᵗʰ   I have peace this morning and heath *(health)*. met in peace a very hot day, at night a very tremenduous Cloud arose, and for about one hour a constant lightning without much intermission, and loud thunder and rain. Yet I have a god to depend on.

6ᵗʰ   This morning Cloudy. yet have health and Consolation. meet in peace. tis our day of prayer meeting. we met, a good number came, but O how dead   how lifeless we are.

7ᵗʰ   Meet this morning in peace. tis a fine morning   last night O what Strugles, *(struggles)* weak faith. lifles *(lifeless)* and dull we met and parted. We have been too unfaithfull here, O for help from on high my Lord.

8ᵗʰ   fine morning. but I now am in pain as I was when So Sick. I submit to the Lords will. I know nothing can hurt me then. I will rejoice in God my Savior and will Submit my cause to the Saviour of my Soul.

9ᵗʰ   A day of labour at home. a very hot day indeed a day of painfull feeling to me.

10ᵗʰ   Sabbath this is a day of great exercise, I am disappointed from Class meeting and go to Tignels but I am disappointed truly return, am truly dull, and lifeless determined to be more engaged. Lord help me.

11ᵗʰ   Cloudy day, meet in peace   full School am in trouble this morning Matilda and family arrive, from Oglethorpe. Cloudy and wett weather.

12ᵗʰ   Dark morning. I am here and a few with me but O how fallen from that life That power I once enjoyed. I lament that I make so little progress in religion. I give way too much to false reasoning. Lord undertake for me and relieve me from unbelief. I pray.

13ᵗʰ   Wet and Cloudy day. meet many come. feel better in Soul this morning. O for more Life of religion. last night was dull.

14ᵗʰ   Last night we had prayer meetg. *(meeting)* an *(d)* a comfortable time we had but no noise. This is a fair fine morning. yesterday we had much rain. O I do not feel as I wish Yet am I in faith and hope. O may this be a day of Joy.

15ᵗʰ   A fair day. we are met   many meet but tis a day of trial. I have not that faith I wish. many are the hindrances we meet this morning yet I feel on my way.

16ᵗʰ   A day of labour at home. many are my trials. yet many are my mercies.

17ᵗʰ   Sabbath. I go to Camp meeting in Oglethorpe County. tis a fine day. I arrive about 11ᵗʰ hour. hear much good preaching.

hear 3 Sermons See much work of God among the people yet not as great as I have Seen   people are very *(sickly ?)* indeed   great work this night. till day break I sleep   none that I know of.

18ᵗʰ   Monday. This morning I feel too dull   we had a good time at the holy Sacrament. I have had some faint: refreshing. I have once morng. *(more)* renewed my Covenant to be the Lord's. I return home. tis thought 22 were converted. 17 Join Society. Supposed 50 mourners & Converts this mo. *(month ?)* find all well at home . . .

19ᵗʰ   Meet the School in peace but few, hear of the death of my neighbour's death which I hope will alarm the neighborhood. Lord help me.

20ᵗʰ   Meet in peace and quiet. Sickness begins to rage. O may the people learn righteousness and truth.

21ˢᵗ   last night we had a happy time in prayer meeting. many were made happy and I hope good was done. my Soul draws nigher to god. Lord help me to advance   This evening a dark cloud rises, it rains and a tremendous Storm.

22ⁿᵈ   fine morning, few scholars. I have a hard Struggle this morning. O for more religion and happiness.

23ʳᵈ   This morning I am home at work   a comfortable day. how watchfull ought I to be in the things of god and religion I find much to **(unk.)** my Soul is lifted above but how am I tried on every hand. Lord help me now.

24ᵗʰ   Sabbath. Class meeting at bro. *(bro. marked through)* meeting house. tis a good day to me and many Souls. yet I feel Some heaviness at night. O when Shall I gain an entire Victory over Sin. my Saviour I look to thee.

25th Meet in peace this morning a number of Scholars. a day of peace to me yet have I trials.

26th fine morning to my Soul but alas I was unguarded last night to my Soul it was a good day but I was led to Speak too trifling and felt Condemned, this morning I was too fretfull in my family.

27th Meet in peace. fine morning I now have hope yet I have Trials. this night is our prayer meeting. I hope for a great meeting.

28th last night was our prayer meeting Some Strangers were here, and we had a comfortable waiting on God but no visible work. O I long to be wholly given up to God. Lord help me. I pray.

29th This morning is Cloudy we have been favoured with a good time for getting fodder I am not Clear as I wish to be.

30th A day of labour at home. rainy and a day of trial an *(d)* trouble. O I am dull and heavy a day of great trials inwardly.

31st Sabbath: I Stay at home and am indeed lifeless. Lord undertake for me O when shall I gain a nearer approach to god and be whole. I am overcome by anger.

1st **September.** Meet in peace. I am too lifeless. O what a day of inward Trial and fear, and grief.

2nd fine morning. meet in peace I did feel a nearness to god this morning in private prayer.

3rd Cloudy day all is not well with me. I am weak as a Child in religion, tis our prayer meeting night. O for a great times, indeed.

4th last night we had a great time of love in prayer meeting: Many were here and I hope good was done.

5th Meet in peace and quiet. now I am not as I wish to be. in **(unk.)** heaviness too much for trifles. Lord help me to revive and live to thee.

6th At home, a day of labour, and pain yet am I supported   O for a closer walk with god   a calm repose in christ   I have felt this evening greater degree of confidence in my Saviour and have been much blessed. O my Soul wait upon God in earnest   he will uphold thee and keep thee Safely through all thy Sorrows and bring thee to Glory.

7th Sabbath: no Meeting, and I am here alone. I have this morning been wrong   I have spoken unadvisedly and did watch as I ought but tis my firm resolve to live for god altogether. I would not offend him willingly. O for faith to do better. Lord be mine.

8th faith is mine. this morning: fair day fine weather. we have had some little sickness but all are recovering   bless the Lord O my Soul. meet in peace.

9th fine morning. meet in peace. last night I had a delightful dream, I was at a meeting and some man was powerfully converted, and I was much interested and Shouted so loud it waked me. O how happy I felt. a great meeting.

10th rainy morning indeed   met few Scholars. my wife I left sick this morning   I fear for her but I know my Lord will do right in all things.

11th last night we met in prayer meeting and a great time we had   one Soul professes Conversion Since last meeting. I had views of God thist *(this)* night as I never had. meet in peace, my wife is better.

12ᵗʰ   I am afflicted with a Cold and am very unwell yet am I here very Cloudy I am pestered with various temptations. Lord help me.

13ᵗʰ   A day of labour at home great trials indeed O for help from

14ᵗʰ   Sabbath. Again a Silent Sabbath I am much blest, today Yet am I unwell and tried Lord help me to do better.

15ᵗʰ   Cloudy and wett O for more life   A day of pain to mind and body.

16ᵗʰ   Meet in peace, yet sick. my mind confused yet I have hope in God a day of pain and trials.

17ᵗʰ   I go to meeting am tried, and do and say wrong O for power tis our prayer meeting and we meet. but alas how dull and dead.

18ᵗʰ   Meet in peace. fine day I am very unwell and have Some Trials indeed but not Serious.

19ᵗʰ   fine morning. meet Safely but alas what Struggles have I to undergo my Dreams too disturb me, but why Should I fear, I am Safe in the hands of God and nothing Can hurt me.

20ᵗʰ   Day of labour at home of trial and danger and woe O What deadness I feel and what a lack of wisdom O What would I not give to be free from this dire and doleful feeling Lord deliver me from this unbelief and these Doubts and fears.

21ˢᵗ   Sabbath. Meeting at W. Vitle: dead lifeless. Cold.

22ⁿᵈ   Cloudy   meet Safely   very dull and lifeless in Soul   O when Shall I be free, I know tis my wish to be holy.

23ʳᵈ   Cold and Cloudy weather—O I am yet heavey *(heavy)* lifeless   my Daughter Spencer goes home today.

24ᵗʰ   Cold and damp. but my Soul is yet dull   cast down, heavy. Oh: Oh.

25ᵗʰ   last night we had a good prayer meeting. happy time   Day of trial of heaviness indeed.

26ᵗʰ   this is our day of examination   few children. but they have imp*(roved)* much in few months.

27ᵗʰ   of labour at home   a day of Trial and trouble. many sore temptations. O Lord undertake for us. I pray thee for us.

28ᵗʰ   *(the 28ᵗʰ is scratched through as if the intention was to continue the entry of the 27ᵗʰ)* for me and my family and   O Suffer us not to be tempted more than we can bear I pray. I had Yesterday an examination of the Children and was so pleased with their progress   Yet all will not do unless I can get these parents to do more at him *(home)* for these Children. much of their due improvement depends on the management at home.

28ᵗʰ   Sabbath. this day I appointed to begin a school at the school house but I fear this people will not Send their children to learn. 3 only have come as yet.

29ᵗʰ   Yet I am here in peace   yesterday was a day of trial to me O for more of life of religion in my Soul.

30th   this day is cold. I am here very few scholars tis a morning of trial to me O my Lord.

1st   **September** *(scratched through)* a day of **October**. a day of labour at home and of trial. Lord when Shall I overcome all and be free from Sin and darkness trials I have –

2nd   *(torn)* Meet in peace. Yesterday morning was frost. Cold this morning   prayer meeting this *(scratched through)* last night very few dull and lifeless –

3rd   rainy dark weather and O my Soul how dark how dull. O this morning I Spoke rashly.

4th   a Day of labour at home a time of trouble and pain many mercies I enjoy at home.

5th   I enjoy great priviledges Why am I thus. O my Soul I have not that faith I wish I love God but alas how Cold my love I have not that faith I wish nor thaat *(that)* light I want O wh *(torn – when)* Shall I be delivered.

Fourth Section

This section is on the same size paper with borders lined as the 2ⁿᵈ section. It begins on what should have been 3-5-1828 and continues through 8-10-1828. On occasion, one entry is continued in the next day's entry. Since most are uniform entries on particular places of the pages, it suggests that the writer lined off the dates prior to filling in comments, as if to save paper or to limit himself to a phrase or two per entry. The left hand side of each sheet begins with the Sabbath, allotting only the space of two page sides to contain a week's entries.

The problem with dating the first entries of this section comes on the first day marked the **26ᵗʰ** (which should have been 3-26-1828). In that entry, Andrew wrote: "I have kept no regular Journal from this Day till I begun School on 14ᵗʰ January..." It is unclear if the first fragment of the month was indeed March, 1828, or if Andrew wrote in another month on previously dated blank sheets.

The entry of the 21ˢᵗ suggests that the beginning of this section was from 12-5-1827 through the end of that month, picking back up on 4-6-1828. The entry reads: "Farewell now for a while I am no more here till after Christmas. And now I have Concluded another year in this. . .School." Perhaps there was a skip from 1-1-1828 – 4-5-1828 when Andrew wrote nothing.

5ᵗʰ   last night I had a night meeting at Bro. Wrights. we had a good time, precious Season of love. Lord water the Seed Sown.

6ᵗʰ   This morning I am hoarse unwell. as of Yet God is mine. I enjoy his love but I long to be filled: O for more.

7th   last night we had prayer meeting a comfortable time of Joy: few only Came. I feel this morning very hoarse indeed. but I will

8th   go on: a Day of trial at home Adieue *(Adieu)* for this week.

9th   Sabbath: This morning I am much better while yesterday I was very Sick. last night I had a very Comfortable meeting indeed.

10th   Yesterday was Sabbath School. I was better today is Preaching here I hope for a good time indeed There is now a good prospect.

11th   Yesterday we had a good time at Sacrament we had two new members Joined us and many more I hope will do it soon.

12th   Yesterday was rainy. this is fair and Cold. I was in great pain from midnight, am now better but yet in pain of body.

13th   This morning I am better but Still in pain of body. Yet I enjoy peace of Soul: tis Cloudy.

14th   Tis fair no rain. I Came last night but two here Oh what times among us. Lord revive us. Glory to God forever that

15th   we are no worse. I will hope even against hope. amen.

16th   Sabbath: Yesterday and this day our meeting was here bros. Stanly and Barnet are present Great and good meeting especially at Sacrament. 75 commune.

17th   Yesterday was a good time. Yet I fell badly I have been unfaithful and unholy I long for more holiness of heart and am resolved to obtain more religion.

18th last night I was overtaken by Gloom and Spoke rashly in my family. O how I regret having done so. I would be humbled in the very dust before God for my Sinfulness and Shame.

19th last night I preached at bro. Wrights many came and we had a good meeting Wm. Wrigghts meet house burnt up much in it. poor Souls.

20th Yesterday my wife went to Leonards and I am left alone feel pained much in body.

21st Farewell now for a while I am no more here till after Christmas. And now I have Concluded another year in this

22nd School. I have much to praise my God for, and much to blush for.

23rd Sabbath a Day of peace how much have I to be thankfull to my Lord and Master – Yet I am often wandering.

24th This is a day of labour of trial of love, of Joy. of trials many. Yet I am able to Conquer by the grace of my Lord. O for more faith and

25th This day I am rejoicing at the thought of my dear and blessed Saviours Death and Sufferings.

26th I have kept no regular Journal from this Day till. I begun school on 14th January Various are my trials. many blessings are given

27th me I have generally had 2 night meetings in the week often 3 I hope good has been done.

28th I long for a gracioius revival of thy work here O Lord send us help from on high   tis time to work my Lord for

29th   many have made Void thy Law   my adored Lord and Saviour.

Note: 16th Brother Barnet was likely William B. Barnett who had served the Appalachee Circuit in 1818 and who had located in 1821. In this late time (1828), Andrew was living in the area where he was buried near Mt. Zion Church, Oconee County.

6th   **April: 1828.** Sabbath. I am here this morning but not at home, came last night to Reas *(?)*

7th   Spent an agreeable night. go this *(scratched through)* last morning to Rehoboth have few but have good meeting. Come home

8th   Yesterday I went to Court house on buisness. *(business).* return am unwell, have a Combatt with

9th   John Davenport. I have been Much blessed in Preaching and in private prayer: bless God.

10th   last night we had a meeting at my house. bro. Oliver preached   a good meeting: Yet I felt bad O for more religion more love.

11th   I feel this morning that I love my God. Yet I have not that Joy   I wish to live for God altogether   Give me Lord to feel always

12th   Wen*(t)* last night to bro. Huntons had full house great liberty and a good meeting rode to town. and home again.

13th   Sabbath: I am here felt well this morning no one com*(es)* rainy great blessing has been frost about the 2nd this month Killed all vegetation. even leaves on the trees.

14th   I was very much sick last night. I am so now but I am here. Yesterday we had a glorious meeting and I felt much in the meeting. a great one indeed.

15th   I am here very unwell and can hardly attend to the School yet I feel a Confidence of my title to Heaven through my blessed Lord. O for more faith.

16th   This morning I am better. In Soul I am confident and happy I love God. I however have Some trials. but God is good Lord undertake for me now.

17th   Rainy great blessing. I am very unwell Yet the Lord does the lord blesses me, and mine   O for more religion of Soul.

18th   I am truly unwell, Yet I have Confidence in God and love him Sincerely. O help me.

19th   This is the first Day of our meeting I am not able to go Sick I am indeed Lord help me now.

20th   Sabbath: Today I did not Go to love feast: they had a good one I am here at preaching Good sermon and exhortation. I feel will *(well?)* but no Work among

21st   This day I am here I am better in health than Yesterday. in Soul I am too lifeless Lord undertake for me I pray and make me holy.

22nd   I was Sick this morning and Oh I was overtaken this morning with this horrid gloom. I Spoke wrong and felt wrong I grieved my family Lord help me to amend my manner of life. Lord help.

23rd last night I was blest but O what I have Suffered for two days last past: my Soul has groaned under trials my body under pain. Lord heal me.

24th I am happily favoured last night with Sisters Stewart and martin from Green. and have much enjoyment.

25th This morning is Cloudy. I am unwell. Yet I love God and feel my acceptance with my God. Lord may I never depart.

26th the greatest hail today I ever Saw and Storm. yet all is Safe I am unwell Judy is Sick.

27th Sabbath: Circuit Preaching we had a good time indeed I felt much in Class meeting. O for a great revival of the work of God among us.

28th This morning my Soul has enjoyed much and last night. I am better in health. Judy is Yet sick. but I think better.

29th Thank my Lord my Judy is better this morning. I am very unwell. but in Soul I am well. O: for more religion. O for holiness of Soul.

30th This morning my Soul is well. tis the last day of the month Yet I am not as much filled as I wish.

Notes: **6th** A church in Oconee County with a deed record from Clarke County in 1842 was Ray's. This may be the Reas that Andrew referred to which may have been called Rehoboth at that time. **9th** John Davenport ? **10th** bro. Oliver was possibly John L. Oliver who was on the Grove Circuit in 1828.

1st   **May.** This day I am Suddenly called to marry Frank Oliver to mary love and return to meeting at bro. Olivers Where we have a great meeting.

2nd   This is fast day to us. bro Oliver preaches and we have a melting time among us.

3rd   This is a day of labour and sorrow but I am brought through.

4th   Sabbath: I am here tis bro. Alexanders Day. We have a hope of a good meeting. Lord be with us.

5th   Yesterday I was greatly blessed We had a great Class meeting and a good prayer meeting.

6th   Rainy how great a blessing to us. Nature Smiles man rejoices.

7th   Rains incessantly. I have this morning Eternity near in View.

8th   I have a witness in my Soul that God is my all in all.

9th   I have this morning a blessing from Heaven in prayer. Yet how backward fair weather this morning. O for more love.

9th   *(appeared as 10th, then altered).* last night I was at night meeting at bro. Oliver. he preached some were moved and I hope good was done. I am happy and confidt. *(confident)* Lord help me to live right.

10th   This is a day of trials and pains Yet mercy crowns my days but I am unfaithfull.

11th   Sabbath: I preach at Rehoboth many People   tis a dull time   I am trifling   I feel that I have erred   Lord help me.

12th   This morning I am dull and too lifeless   I long to be more devoted to God in good earnest.   I felt Condemned for too much trifling.

13th   I have been blessed with love.   O I have been long dull and lifeless State   O may I never do So any more, Keep me O my dear Redeemer in peace.

14th   I long to be free from all Sin   O my Lord thou knowest my Soul   I long for full Salvation   I feel yet some besetting Sins.

15th   Cool. I am not Clean in heart   I feel much in me Contrary to Religion   I want a deeper work in my Soul   Lord undertake.

16th   I am now better and feel in hope of heaven and glory   O for more religion: Lord

17th   A day of fatigue and pain.

18th   Sabbath: We had today a good Sermon and a glorious day   May my Lord bless the word   the people were much moved.

19th   I am dull and lifeless   my Soul is heavy. I did wrong yesterday evening. Lord help me to do that which wright *(right)* I would be

20th   holy. Rainy. I am much blessed in prayer last night. I now feel how great a matter it is to keep a pure Conscience. a very small deviation gives pain to the Soul   a little matter causes darkness to the Soul: Lord help me.

21st This morning I am unwell I had a good meeting last night at brother wrights	returned home	felt well indeed. Lord help me.

22ⁿᵈ	I had a pleasant night and am now well in body and happy in Soul for God is mine.

23ʳᵈ	I am blessed of the Lord greatly	Yet have I not that Sweet fulness I wish. greatly I long for a revival of the work

24ᵗʰ	of God among us. this is a day of labour. I have a night meeting at bro. Olivers.

25ᵗʰ	**Sabbath** This morning I go to Salem	we have many people	a good love feast	good time at Sacrament: good sermon but

26ᵗʰ	no stirr: I return this morning	we have a great time. O I feel as if if the work will revive here	the enemy has strove hard here to destroy us and if my Lord does not

27ᵗʰ	Interpose we are lost fore ever *(forever)*	I am here this morning in good health and my family also	I was much blessed this morning in Reading the Bible	I pray that I may love to read more O Lord help me: I pray.

28ᵗʰ	This morning I am happy	I had a good meeting last night at Wrights. here Closes my night meetings till next winter:

29ᵗʰ	I am early Called to: counteract the evill between bros. Graves and Wright. I hope to have all right. Lord help us.

30ᵗʰ	It rains yet I am here. very few as yet. I feel determined to pursue holiness with every power	I am not holy	I want to be dead to Sin.

31ˢᵗ   A day of labour toil and pain I go to an appointment this evening at bro. Huntons. Lord Go with me   Lord. or all is vain.

Note: 4ᵗʰ Bro. Alexander was likely William Alexander (1802-1845) who was without a traveling appointment between 1826 and 1830. Alexander had married Mary M. Blanton (1805-1840), a daughter of Rev. Benjamin Blanton. Both were natives of Oglethorpe County. Alexander pastored the Grove Circuit in 1831, the year following Andrew's death. **25ᵗʰ** The Salem mentioned was a church then in SE Clarke County, Oconee County after 1875. It began in 1820 in the little town called Candy. By 1837, it was on the Watkinsville Circuit.

1ˢᵗ   **June:** Sabbath: I am at Rehoboth have a good meeting I dine at Rays come and hear: bro. Hays. then home preached at Huntons   a good

2ⁿᵈ   time: This morning is Cloudy and I hope for rain Lord help me   we need it much. our fields are Suffering for want of rain   But alas we are in an awful Situation in Society O Lord.

3ʳᵈ   I am not as holy as I wish to be   I do not enjoy God as I wish to be   I long to be entirely given up to God in heart and in life   I am too lifeless. Lord revive me I pray you.

4ᵗʰ   This is a day of Trial to me   fair and warm no rain, we suffer   everything droops. and suffers. Yet God is good and gracious to me   my Soul is happy this morning.

5ᵗʰ   My Soul is heavy and longs to be free from Sin of every kind I hate all Sin. O for more humility Lord make me holy in heart   an *(?)*.

6ᵗʰ   Tis dry weather we suffer   O what great distress was *(was marked through)* we Suffer God but withholds his mercy Grant me Lord a greater engagemet *(engagement)*.

7th Tis a day of labour at home and many troublesome went to meetg. at Watkinsville. Dull time.

8th Sabbath: I am here this morning. I would have gone to Rehoboth but I am obliged to be at our own meeting her *(here)* today my children are gone to meeting.

9th Yesterday Bro. Pope preached a good Sermon here. we had a good Class meeting but I felt bad. O that I Could do

10th better: Still dry. Crops are lost with *(without?)* rain Shortly, Yet I believe we shall have it shortly, I was much blessed this morning in reading the Scriptures. O that I Could love it more than ever.

11th Thank my God we have had a good rain I felt well this morning reading the Scripture. Lord let me love it more than ever. to need it.

12th This mornings reading was much blest to me. it was in Hannahs prayer for Samuel She gave him to god, and I did my James. both

13th we accepted: O how good my dear Lord is this morning in reading my Soul was blerssed. O my Lord

14th give me thy love. I am this day happy. Yet I have many troubles but God is my friend. I Shall be delivered from all.

15th Sabbath: We are here this morning we have a good meeting we are much blessed tis a great day many are blesst, at prayer meeting few Came out: Close in great peace.

16th This day I am in Confidence Yet O why am I so dull, so very lifeless in religion: I want to be all alive to god and his people.

17th I am happy I am blest in my Soul in my family God is mine I am his: I have this morning happy yet I had a view of my past life what a Sinner was I what mercy divine that I should be spared.

18th Yesterday was a day of trial to me a day of Sorrow I am now unwell in body Yet am here: Yesterday I was bountifully Supplied with corn.

19th Yesterday I was mercifully provided with money though my foolish heart Lord undertake for me give me to feel thy love.

20th This morning my Soul was blesst in reading the Bible. O I am greatly Blessed of

21st the Lord. This is a day of trouble and Sorrow. trial Yet am I supported in my trials and pains God is mine and I am his.

22nd Sabbath: I went this day to Watkensville and preached to about thirty. Oh how fallen are these.

23rd Meet in peace this day. fair morng. we have had a famous rain to *(scratched out).* O how good the Lord is to us Crops are truly promising to us.

24th Yesterday we had a glorious time happy day: we had 3 babtist *(baptist)* preachers but bro. Ray preached a good sermon.

25th My wife has been Sick but my Lord has healed her Thanks to his holy name. I was blessed this morng. in private prayer and in readg. the Scripture: Glory to God.

26th   last night we had a great rain   a blessing indeed. This morning we had a cloudy wet morning my Soul rejoices in god. I have faith in Jesus.

27th   Long let me adore that hand that Redeemed me and Saved my Soul from woe. O may I not depart from my Lord and master this day I love my God.

28th   This is a day of triall and Sorrow of labour O may I love my Lord I have some trials, but many blessings, I am at home I was to have gone to Rays to a two day *(meeting?)* but am disappointed.

29th   Sabbath: I am here at the Sabbath School and though I wished to have been at Rays today. Yet as I believe. I am in the order of God. I Submit Cheerfully. I am blessed.

30th   I am blessed in Reading this morng. my Soul yesterday in Class meeting I am happy in God. I long to be swallowed up in love Lord to me make known thy

Notes: 9th Bro. Pope was Benjamin Blanton Pope (1804 – 1835), son of Henry Pope, Sr., who was on the Appalachee Circuit in 1828-29.

1st   **Day July:** O may I begin a new life with a new Week. last night I felt the Lord very near to me. tis a great thing to be a true Christian.

2nd   I had a good time in private and in family prayer at brother Olivers he is at home. and improes *(improves?)* and is a man of excellent Spirit. O for a closer walk with god a

3rd   This morning is very cool. I have been out of my usual order and am lifeless I gave way to a wrong temper.

4ᵗʰ   very Cool weather this morning   I was blessed this morning in prayer   my Soul loves God but not enough   Oh for perfection   O for holiness.

5ᵗʰ   a day of labour at home   of pain and Joy   love and peace to my Soul. I am unwell.

6ᵗʰ   Sabbath: I preach at rehoboth. good meeting: here bro. pope at four at Mt. Zion:

7ᵗʰ   We had a good meeting. bro. Pope stays with me   he is a good preacher. O for a Closer walk with God thro. **(unk.)** this day.

8ᵗʰ   I have many trials this morng. *(morning)* Oh I am unclean unholy   Lord help me. I pray. I here have felt an evidence of my acceptance and am Confident in my evidence   O for more religion real heart felt religion.

9ᵗʰ   This morning my Soul was blest   Yet my Lord give me more religion   I long to be entirely filled. O I want the spirit of Devotion.

10ᵗʰ   This morning my Soul is too dull and lifeless. I have Confidence I have have hope   I have love

11ᵗʰ   last night I was much blest   this morning I am blest. my Lord is near me. he has heard me and has healed Caroline. Glory to his

12ᵗʰ   Name I have this day trials and Crosses and many favours.

13ᵗʰ   Sabbath: I am here to the Sunday School   no one here yet. but few come   I fear for this School. O my Lord   Save us my Savior.

14th   We had but 6 at Class meeting Oh I fear for The Society here. Cold lifeless Sinful O lord revive us   we have many faithful ones.

15th   last evening and this morning I was much blest in private prayer I have every day proof of the goodness of God to my Soul Lord undertake for me.

16th   I am too dull this morning yet I am much blessed in prayer O that I Could feel every day the presence of my Lord God.

17th   Dull and lifeless this morning I am unwell all the morning. Yet O how unshaken my hope.

18th   This morning has been gloomy to me. Yet I had Some faint smile   Oh I am unfaithfull to god..

19th   I am here yet but few are come   I fear for this School. O my Lord and master …

20th   Sabbath: few met at the School: we had a good meeting I was happy, yet interrupted by Company in the evening much.

21st   This has been a day of blessing we have *(it has)* been a day of great things O for a heart of Gratitude to my Lord for I have many blessings at home and in Zion.

22nd   This morning my soul is good for nothing. Dull lifeless: heavy tis a very Dry time no rain for many weeks. Corn is now suffering.

23rd   This morning my my Soul has but a faint Glimpse of Joy Yet I am happy in his love who died to save me from sin.

24th   last evening bro. Bellah was with us   we had a good meeting Lord help us to improve all.

25th   We had rain last evening but Still we want more. O what are we if God witholds the rain this more *(morn)* I am too dull.

26th   A day of Sorrow toil and pain I have Company. I am not well.

27th   Sabbath: I have a good meetg. at School house. some feeling but alas how fallen this Society. Yet is there hope for it.

28th   This morning I am too dull and lifeless. School is full O for more Religion now to be forever blest in good earnest my soul love*(s)* God.

29th   I have had the greatest trials last night O my Soul what a night of trial and pain. what struggles. I spoke wrong I did wrong I thought wrong Pain plenty we have had.

30th   This morning my Soul has been somewhat blessed, more than I deserve Lord help me to do bettter O I would pass another such trial.

Notes: 24th Bro. Bellah was either James Bellah who was on the Appalachee Circuit in 1825 and the Walton Circuit in 1828-29 or Morgan Bellah who did not enter the traveling connection until 1833 when he was appointed to the Grove Circuit. Morgan Bellah was born in Oglethorpe County and could have preached in the area prior to his admission on trial in 1833.

1st   **August:** I am Confident yet not Joyous. but I will be resigned I deserve not even what I have. we have had plenty of rain. Thanks

2ⁿᵈ My Soul last night and this morning has enjoyed much from my lord   to be pure is my wish   O for more true religion. Lord

3ʳᵈ I *(s)*tarted for Walton Camp meeting Got there about ten: find a great work   am Called to exhort. we have a good work here: I am greatly blessed of God.

4ᵗʰ Sabbath: We have a great many people Great preaching a very great work O I rejoice at the prosperty

5ᵗʰ of the work. This morning we part Solemn time   never all to meet again on earth   all of us. 60 convert appeard. O may these all meet at last.

6ᵗʰ I rejoice at the prosperity of the work of the Lord I am much tired with riding to and from the meeting but I am truly Glad I went. I have some trials I am however supported. I feel that I Shall Conquer at last. Lord help me to live holy.

7ᵗʰ Cloudy this morning and warm we hope for rain my Soul now feels a lifeless state O for more real religion at heart Zion mourns here   Lord help.

8ᵗʰ I am yet too dull and lifeless   my Soul is Confident in hope but have not Joy as I wish.

9ᵗʰ This morning I have some trials   Yet I have been blest much in private prayer but not as in days past Lord help me.

10ᵗʰ A day of labour at home   of pain and sorrow trial   joy.

Fifth Section

This section is the only typescript from an original, yet the original was not included. Whoever transcribed it left many words blank and probably made errors in the transcription that cannot be identified. While the outer cover has typed on it, "Diary of John Andrew from November 21, 1826 – ending Leap Year," the second page of the transcription bears the date, July, 1829. The typescript date was an error, for 1828 was the leap year. The journal, then was from 11-21-1828 – 1829.

This morning my soul hath peace. I have my happiest time at night, God helps me in the night season – Glory to God.

21st O Glory to God for all his blessings to me and mine. Last night I had a glorious time.

22nd Rainy and dark yet my soul has peace. I love God, Lord keep me near thy side. I have home trials, am pestered with many things.

29th A day at home, many trials, generally on this day more than all, yet I am preserved admidst and mercy is all through the day.

30th Sabbath: Brother *(blank)* preaches Bro. Alexander exhorts but a dull time to me. Yet have I faith in my Glorious Redeemer.

1st Day of December. I have a dull feeling of Soul and am much pestered with worldly thoughts yet I am blessed from day to day, and have some happy moments, but I *(blank)* to be filled.

2nd   Very cold and fair. My soul is too dull and lifeless. Yet I have a hope beyond the grave. O my Lord help me to be more faithful and be sanctified and sweetly filled with love.

3rd   This day my soul is too dull. I do not enjoy God as I wish. O Lord tis my desire to do thy holy will. I long to do thy holy will in good earnest – save me from all sin and pain.

4th   Today I am truly dull and lifeless. Oh! when shall I overcome all my enemies, and above all my own sinful heart. Lord and Master love me to the end.

5th   This day my soul is full of pain – I do not feel my God enough   tis gloom and sorrow.

6th   Yesterday evening I had a fall and am crippled, am in much pain. I think my rib is broken in my right side.

7th   Sabbath. This day it was hard and I am at home all day in pain of body, but am cheered in Soul; much company and I am *(blank)*.

8th   This morning am here, but my body is much pained. Cloudy, rainy and cold, but in soul I am blessed. Glory be to God, I am happy.

9th   I have had a pleasing prospect of heaven and Glory my Soul rejoices. I am pestered with worldly thoughts and temptations. O that I was holy in heart and life before my God.

10th   Cares come on me on every hand, yet I am delivered and kept secure admidst storms.

11th   This week and last I have had ten scholars, it does appear my day of school is nearly done here, but I shall be provided for somewhere.

12th   I was very sick yesterday, I did not attend. A day of pain in body, but my soul was calm.

13th   This day at home in pain *(blank)* I can't labor. O for resignation to my Lord, will I have a little peace. Jesus is mine.

14th   Sabbath: I am in much pain. I don't go to meeting *(blank)*. Yet I am bright of God. My Lord help me to watch and pray more.

15th   It is now cold and very fair. Such a season of warm weather for the season I never knew. I am in pain and know not the present cause.

16th   I am at home receiving my *(blank)* cool weather. I am still in pain, and not able to do much, yet I feel thankful tis no worse with me. No School till January.

17th   This morning my soul has peace and confidence, but I have not joy, I long to be filled. Lord revive religion among us in earnest. Keep us by the.

19th   July, 1829

19th   July. Sabbath: This is Bro. Alexander's day here. I feel revived in soul in some degree. O for a fullness of love.

20th   Cloudy this morning, appearance of rain. Fine crops of corn and cotton, but my soul thou cheered and confident in hope yet dull.

21st   O Lord banish from us as a family everything that offends. May we seek more religion and serve thee more truly than ever we did *(blank)* Lord I have strong hope.

22nd   Today I am in confidence, but I long to be made holy. I know that Jesus is mine and I am his today.

23rd   This morning I have a blessing. I feel I am hastening to the grave. O for more life in religion, my God make me more holy.

24th   I have been much blest this morning   my soul is free from that loud *(cloud?)* which I have long born.

25th   I go to town, then to Davenport's and tarry all night. I am not well, but hope to be able to keep on.

26th   Sabbath: I preached today at the schoolhouse. We had a good meeting, dined with Ojsitun Apling, rode home.

27th   This morning I am happy, but do not feel that flow of love. I long for love, grant me this, thy salvation fully, thy holy spirit entirely my.

28th   Today it rains after a long dry spell, how pleasing, how gracious is our God. O may I serve thee more faithfully. I wish to be everyday alive to God and religion.

29th   Fine rain last night. Nature is revived, great crops of corn every where.

30th   Fair today. I am confident, yet I feel not that flow of love which I wish to enjoy. Yet I will try to live by faith. Lord help me to pray and praise.

31st This morning, O what sore trials have I met. Lord help. Fine rain yesterday indeed. O could I live more devoted.

1st **August:** This day at home of labor and trials, another month is gone.

2nd Sabbath: This my day here O Lord help me to preach for if thou help not all will be vain *(blank)* a word today.

3rd Yesterday we had a dull time, few people. I did feel badly thru the day my soul mourned. I did feel unhappy indeed.

4th Last night I was blessed much. This morning I am in faith, but I had a painful night in body. The family is unwell.

5th Rainy, cloudy this morning. I have full confidence in God. I long for pefect love. Lord give me.

6th This morning is cloudy – great rains yesterday indeed. My soul is confident in home, but I have not perfect love. I have not that joy I wish.

7th I am happy this morning my soul rejoices in love. I have the smile of my Saviour, this is enough. All are recovering now.

8th My wife and Tutsy started yesterday for Athens with James. I have had a blessed day in private all praise to my Lord God, I am happy.

9th Sabbath: Pope's Day in the evening. Lord send a good day. We have good preachers, but no revival among us.

10th O what a sudden change from being happy to a state of dullness and the *(blank)* O my Lord undertake for me.

11th This is a previous morning to me yet I have trials many. O how I long to be free from sin and to be entirely holy.

12th Last night my son came to us – he had a good meeting at Athens; joined two men *(blank)* My own soul is confident yet too dull.

13th I have been too far from God, my Soul has been too lifeless yet am I confident knowing that Jesus is mine and I am his. I long to be entirely free from sin.

14th I am in a strange way. Some days I am greatly blessed of God and enjoy much and then I am dull and lifeless, yet I have a sure witness of my acceptance with God.

15th I am at home tis a day of trial. We have much company. Tis a day of confusion, very hot. My soul has peace and a confident hope, but confusion and not well. O for more religion.

16th Sabbath: We have here preaching by Bro. Williams and Wright, but we are finding very dull time indeed. Company in evening, but all are gone.

17th My wife is gone too and left me for a season. Lord make me better every day.

18th This morning it rains constant. I am here about twelve in soul, I feel better but O I long to be filled with love and joy O my divine Lord fill me. I pray thee thy love is precious indeed.

19th Rain incessant – no school. I did not come, my soul is at too great a distance from God yet I enjoy a firm peace of Soul. O for more religion.

20th This day. I am here and have found a blessing to my soul.

Yet this morning have I had some trials and did not stand fast as ought.

21st   Still cloudy no rain of account. My soul is heavy I have not joy. I wish but I have great peace.

22nd   Tis a day of trial and pain, but innumerable mercies are given us as a family.

23rd   Sabbath: I go this morning to school house and preach to a number of people from, "Ye must be born again." We had a tender time indeed.

24th   Ride from Davenport's this morning, am much overcome indeed. Yesterday I was truly overcome. I am indeed unwell, but was blessed yesterday, and am today.

25th   I am here and but one scholar. Sickly about here, fine fair weather for getting fodder. I never knew greater crops made.

26th   This morning is cloudy and rainy yet I am here with one scholar. In soul I have peace and uncommon liberty in *(blank)*.

27th   A rainy day yesterday – fodder I fear ruined. Many people will have all lost, but the will of God be done. I am safe in his love.

28th   Cloudy, fodder lost I fear. I have been blessed and have a firm peace of soul, but not that joy I wish. Lord fill me with love.

29th   A day at home   of home trials, but of great blessings to my soul and to my family.

30th   Sabbath: Yesterday and this morning fair and dry. I was pleading for all sin to be taken away, and it appeared to me all was good.

31ˢᵗ   Yesterday Bro. Hays preached. We had a great day, I was happy and many of the brethren felt, O that it may be the beginning of a Glorious revival among us.

Note: **16ᵗʰ** Bro. Williams was probably William S. Williams who served the Appalachee Circuit in 1827. He was appointed to Gwinnett in 1828 and to Habersham in 1829-30. While Bro. Wright is not identified, he could have been John C. Wright, local preacher, who located in 1829 or Stephen Wright (1798-1862) who married in Greene Co., GA in 1813 and for whom there is no conference record. **31ˢᵗ** Bro. Hays was probably William Hays, a local preacher who married Nancy Halchet of Oglethorpe County in 1819 and who was elected an elder in 1832.

1ˢᵗ   **September:**   Last night we had a tremendous thunderstorm. This morning I had sweet converse with my God, Glory be to God   I am happy in his love, yet I long for more religion.

2ⁿᵈ   Fair this day. This morning I had too much unbelief, yet I had a comfortable waiting upon God – Lord keep me this day.

3ʳᵈ   I had a restless night until this morning, but I was blessed in prayer in the night. I have a firm hope beyond this world of woe. O for more religion.

4ᵗʰ   Very cold this morning and fair. I was blessed this morning in private, but O I want to be full of love and peace.

5ᵗʰ   A day of labor at home   trials and many blessings – thanks my God for all things.

6th   Sabbath: This day was Class *(meeting)*, but I was so sick I did not go home   met, but no meeting. I am pained for fear I have done wrong, forgive me Lord.

7th   This day is Brother Pope's day. Many come and we have a good meeting. O I hope to be happy in a great revival of religion, Lord send it.

8th   Yesterday I am much blessed in meeting, today I am not well. Yet I am here with only one scholar. Lord prepare me to do and suffer all   thy holy will I pray.

9th   Very cold this morning and no scholar as yet, O what a time to me. I see no way for a *(a struck though)* provisions for the family, but I know my Lord will point out some way.

10th   New trials are prepared for me, but grace I hope has enabled me to overcome. I have no school this morning, but it matters not   I am in the house of my God.

11th   No school, I am here   Brother Oliver has visited us and we have had a glorious time together and I glory to God for all his kindness.

12th   A day of sickness and trials.

13th   Sabbath: Still cold and dry. I am here, but only four persons come to Class meeting – a day of sickness to me, yet peace of soul. O for a fullness.

14th   This morning is cold – no rain. Crops of corn are great, but no cotton, the worm is in it much. Had an awful night and little sleep, still I am sick.

15th Last night my son came and we had a happy evening together. My soul this morning is lifeless, but I have a sure confidence in God. I have a hope beyond this world.

16th I am here as usual with one scholar. Sick and lifeless, yet I have hope that the world can never take away.

17th Last night I was careless of my duty at my usual time and this morning the enemy got the advantage. I spoke rashly.

18th I had awful dreams last night, and broken slumber. This morning I have home trials, and O how I feel.

19th At home, a day of sickness and labor, yet how many mercies. Lord undertake for me today.

20th Sabbath: I don't go. Bro. Alexander preaches. They have a happy meeting.

21st Bro. Howard preaches and in Class we have a good time indeed; two joined us. Lord be pleased to keep them faithful – revive us O Lord.

22nd This morning my soul enjoys peace, but not filled with joy. I enjoy much and am blessed, but I long for full redemption in my Saviour's blood. I think this is the beginning of a revival among us here.

23rd This morning I feel a union, but I long to love God with all my heart.

24th Last night was good to me in meditation, but a distress in time in coughing, but why complain, tis my Father's house.

25th This morning I am better, greatly has my cough been stopped. My soul rejoices in God my Saviour. O for more life and love.

26th A day of labor at home. I am very sick and not able to attend my appointment, yet have I great blessings.

27th Sabbath: Meet here for a prayer meeting – ten come. We have a dead cold time. I am very unwell, dull.

28th Cloudy morning, hope for rain – tis a long time since we had rain, very dry and becomming *(second m struck through)* very sickly. I feel this morning a confidence that is firm.

29th I am here, but no scholars. My soul is peace and hope, and now camp meeting comes on. I will write, but little more till tis over.

30th I am here today and feel a firm hope of heaven grounded on the merits of my Saviour. Yet I have not as firm and full *(blank)* of holiness as I wish.

Note: 21st Bro. Howard was John Howard (1792-1836) who served the Appalachee Circuit in 1829-30.

1st **October:** I am at home all this week till Saturday morning, then I go to Camp meeting.

2nd *(blank)* and my soul is happy, and I stay till Sabbath.

3rd Great preaching. My son preaches and Glory to God.

4th Sabbath: This day in exhortation, my soul is sweetly filled. I can't tell what I feel, I come home happy.

5th　　This morning I am still happy in God. Here my journal must cease. I am taken sick and so I continue.

6th　　I am greatly blessed of God from day to day I feel that I cannot remain long and I feel that I have a home beyond this world of sorrow and am hasting to that home.

16th　　I am yet sick, but happy. O for more religion.

17th　　Whats that I render to my God for all his gifts to me. How have I been blessed of my Lord every day in my affliction, but I am not yet sweetly filled as I ought to be, but I look forward with sweet anticipation to the possession of those joys which are eternal.

18th　　Sabbath: Once more I am brought to record the return of the Sabbath of the Lord – don't go to *(to scratched through)* Bro. Wright's preaches, they have a comfortable time I believe.

19th　　This day I go, Bro. Hays does preach, we have rather a dull time. I am yet very unwell indeed. I spoke a little yesterday and I find no hurt.

20th　　I had an awful night and am now very unwell – sick and a fever. O for grace to be patient and resigned to Divine will.

21st　　This morning I felt better, my soul also is blessed. O for more religion, more love to God and his cause.

25th　　I am still sick and able to do very little and that in pain, and Oh I feel too much impatience. O Lord give me that perfect *(blank)* of patience in my soul.

26th　　My son not come. This morning tis rainy. I feel in better health, may I hope to recover strength.

27th   Tis yet cloudy, light rains. My wife and soon *(son?)*, Bro. and sister Grace start for camp meeting in Newton County.

28th   Sabbath: This morning is fair and cool. I have had an awful night, I am weak and much overcome this morning, yet my soul enjoys peace.

(**Note:** There is a date skip here. The 25th is a Sunday in this month, not the 28th).

29th   Today is rainy, a good thing; we have been without a good rain for many months, but now we hope for plenty. I feel better this morning.

28th   I have been very sick this day, but am now better, but I feel I cannot long remain in the body. Lord prepare me.

29th   Cloudy. My wife and son returned last night, all safe. Good time at camp meeting, prospect of great good done.

30th   No rain. Prospect of rainy weather. I am still sick and am much troubled with thought.

31st   Tis to me a sick day, yet I am blessed of God much

1st   **November:** Sabbath. I cannot go to Class meeting – I am blessed at home. Dull meeting I am sick, yet better than I was.

2nd   This morning heavy frost – first we have had this fall. I had a sore night, but am better this morning. I go to preaching this day.

3rd   We had a good sermon by Pope. I felt well. Six persons joined me, among them Hurbert and Mary Spencer. I am much better in health than usual, blessed be my Lord.

4th Still mending yet sick, but also I don't feel that nearness to God I ought. Lord deliver me from sin.

5th Cold and dry   no rain. I have some trials this morning. Yet am I blessed of the Lord. O for more faith, more true religion, more love to God.

6th This morning is rainy and a great blessing. I am truly blessed under Bro. Oliver's prayers. My sickness is more than yesterday. God help me.

7th Fair and cold. Not well. I am very unwell indeed. I am better than I have been. My son is here.

8th Sabbath: This morning I am better in health of body, but too much confused in soul, yet I hope for a good day at Class. Lord help me do just.

9th Today I ride to Bro. Granes. feel better, have a good time in private   this morning in private. O for more true religion at heart.

10th I am better this day in health, yet O how lifeless in soul. I am beset here by many trials. Yet I will try to trust.

11th Very cold this day. This morning we have sleet. I was much blessed in family prayer. I am now sick and suffering, but not much.

12th **Wednesday.** Preparing to start for Greensborough tomorrow. My soul praise God for his goodness.

13th I am doubtful about going, yet I commit all to my Lord. My son comes.

14th We start for *(blank)* have a fatiguing journey, yet we get safe about night.

15th Quarterly meeting begins.

16th Sabbath: Today we have a very good meeting, a great time, a good time indeed. I am pleased and gratified indeed.

17th I am recovered much.

Sixth Section

This final section of the journal provided by Mrs. Earnest is a collection of poems, though it is entitled on the back page, "A Collection of Hymns by John Andrew, 1824. The first 16 of them are enumerated 1-16. It is assumed that they were composed by Andrew. They are listed in the order they appear in the journal section.

Love of God

Love what may well be told of thee,
Thou fairest of the heavenly train:
how charming is thy name to me,
how pleasing is thy heavenly strain
Love moved the Saviour to come down,
To suffer for offending man:
And finish'd, by his death and groan
The great that most sl(*faded*)us plan.
Love Sends the gospel to our ears,
Glad tidings of Salvation brings
Sinners redeemed from Sin and fear
and made to hope for better things.

Contentment

1. Contentment: who with placid eye,
Art Seldom found, yet ever nigh:
Possess me even now.
Then not the Storms that Shake the pole.

Can once disturb my happy Soul,
or ruffle on my brow.

2. Contentment: come in peace arrayed,
And all thy mildest Charms display'd,
And bless my longing eyes:
Thy gentle mein and even pace.
Thy meek regard and heavenly grace
Afford Supreme delight.

3. Contentment: Seal my Souls decree.
To meet my future destiny,
With resignations voice.
Whatever God may let me meet.
May I with resignation Sweet.
Receive and in rejoice.

4. Contenment: *(Contentment)* fairest sweetest plant,
O Lord be pleased the boon to grant,
And let me joyful live:
So when from earth thou Shalt me call
And this my earthly house Shall fall,
Me to thy Joys receive.

Grace: A Poem

1. Grace can unstop the ear that's deaf,
Which long to Sin been a Slave:
Can turn his wicked mirth to grief,
And pluck him from the burning wave.

2. Grace can unseal the blinded eye
That only loves to look at Show:
Can give the Sinner light to Spye
A beauty in religion now.

3. Grace soon can melt the hardest heart,
And cause the tear of Joy to flow:
Can cure the Soul of every Smart.
And give a taste of heaven below.

4. Grace can soon heal the wounded Soul,
And cheer the drooping Spirit too.
Can lead it to the heavenly pool.
And ease the pains of every woe.

5. Grace can destroy the poison here,
Of every Sore, and Sinful dart.
Can take away all pain and fear:
And cure the dreadful, hurtful Smart.

6. Grace can prepare the Saint for heaven
And bring the Soul to joys above,
Lord let thy grace to me be given;
And all my powers be lost in love.

7. Grace gives the dying Saint his Song,
And opens heaven to his View:
The triumphs for his faith is Strong
Then claps his wings and bids, Adieu.

On the Sabbath

1. Once more I hail the day of God,
That day of rest to mortals given;
When Saints go up to hear his word,
And learn the surest way to heaven.

2. Once more within this Silent bower,
Retired, I forget my pains:

No sounds disturb my solemn hour,
None interrupt my plaintive Strains.

3. Once more my powers Shall Join in praise,
To him who gives me power to rise.
In loudest songs my Voice I'll raise
And join the anthems of the skies.

4. Once more to Zions courts, I go,
To hear his word, to sing and pray
The Virtue of his blood to know,
That washes all my sins away.

5. Once and again the gospel sounds
My soul rejoice in Jesus name,
His love to all our race abounds.
Pardon and peace they loud proclaim.

6. Once more the Voice of love I hear
Turn Sinners turn why will ye die.
Fly from your sins forsake your fears,
And on your Savior's word rely.

On the Sabbath

1. Hail holy Sabbath of the Lord,
The day of rest to longing saints.
Thousands go up to hear his word,
And tell their Sorrows and Complaints.

2. Hail day of rest, Sweet Palm of hope
From storms of sin and floods of woe
Peaceful Composure bouys me up
And I to Zion's courts will go.

3. Hail sweet retirement Silent hour
Where oft my Soul of late has been:
How pleasing is this Solemn bower,
Sacred to truth a rapturous Scene.

4. Hail solemn moment of Sweet thought,
When truth can enter and be heard.
Moments of deepest view when nought,
Disturbs my Calm and nought is feared.

5. Hail ye that wait upon the Lord,
In every house in every bower:
Tho far removed ye can afford
By Silent prayer: a Secret power.

6. Hail happy Spirits of the just,
Who sing in Chorus round the throne.
Soon I shall join with you I trust,
To praise the Glorious three in one.

On the duty of ministers

1. Comfort my people saith the Lord of Old,
Yea comfort administer Your Saviour sure has said
Ye prophets who his Sacred word unfold,
And heal the wounds that various Sins have made.

2. Comfort, ye ministers who now do preach,
My Saints Saith Christ; and bind the broken heart
Bear in your arms: those you are sent to teach:
Nor let them long endure Sins cruel Smart.

3. Comfort thro Jesus: flows for every Saint,
If torn by fears, or in temptations Snares

Look unto him by prayer, and never faint
Jesus will save you: then dismiss your fears.

4. Comfort for all, who Sick of Sin are grown
flows from his word, and mercy will be given,
Only repent, and all your follies own,
Believe in Christ, and Claim your right to heaven.

5. Comfort, for all who have their Sins forsaken
And now retrace their former Sinful way
Repent, believe, though you were overtaken
He will forgive, and bring to endless day.

6. Comfort proclaim through Jesus' blood alone,
To rich and poor, to all that do embrace
A full redemption, through his name make known
All may receive, all may obtain his grace.

On the Sabbath

This day, the Saints of God go up,
To Zion's courts to hear his word;
Lord meet us and let a full cup,
Of blessings unto us be pour'd.

2 This day, Lord grant that it may prove,
To Saints who meet on Zion's Hill,
A day of Comfort Joy and Love,
And every jarring note be still.

3 This day: let Sinners feel thy power:
And be resolved to seek the Lord,
O may thy holy Spirit Shower,
Rich blessings by thy holy word.

4 This day may Zion's holy Court,
With joyful Songs resound aloud,
Backsliders fly from guilty sport
And mourners to thy temple Crowd.

5 This day: give ministers new light
Who preach thy word to dying men,
Lord end this scene of war and Strife,
And make all revive again.

6 This day: how mournful is our State,
My Soul would grieve at thy distress,
Who can our miseries relate,
O who will Tell our dolefull Case.

On being reviled

1 When I would gladly be at peace,
And wait in quiet on the Lord:
Many they are who do increase,
My load of woe by lying words.

2 When, to prevent their Shame and pain,
I tell them what I see, that's nought,
My friendly efforts prove but vain,
They seem with angry vengeance fraught.

3 They watch me with an evil eye,
And Strive to prove me false in all.
They still deride as they pass by,
And long to see my fatal fall.

4 I know I am a sinner born,
And most unholy I have been

Yet I no traitor's dress have worn
Nor have I tried my faults to Screen.

5 Lord, give me grace to urge my way,
Thro all the trying scenes of life:
And bring me safe to endless day,
Beyond this world of noise and Strife.

6 Lead me in pastures fresh and green,
O keep me safe from every Snare,
And give me grace to conquer Sin,
Till safe in heaven I all declare.

A view of heaven

1 By faith I see the happy Land
Where all the weary rest,
Fain would my Soul her wings expand,
And fly to Jesus breast.

2 O may I gain that heavenly Shore,
And shun the storms I dread
Where winds and tempests are no more,
Nor waves o'erflow my head.

3 O may thy holy Spirit blow,
Sweet gales of heavenly grace;
And waft me safe from all below
To see my Saviours face.

Advice to Sinners

1 O Sinner from your follies turn,
And Chase those fading forms no more:
Go seek in Solitude to mourn,
And mercy from thy God implore.

2 O may that god whose peircing *(piercing)* eye
Searches the deep retired recess,
To thy diseased Soul draw nigh
And and pity now thy deep distress.

3 Thro all the windings of thy heart,
May grace divine thy searches guide,
And Still his heavenly light impart
Till the whole lump be purified.

The Penitent

1 Hear Lord my humble moan,
O hear my mournful Sighs,
Oh, bid this aful *(awful)* night be gone
And let the dawn arise:

2 O could I make the claim,
My father and my God
And call the *(thee)* mine by that dear name
My Jesus, and my Lord.

3 By every name of love,
I would for light entreat,
And never Should my Soul remove,
Nor leave thy holy Seat.

Retirement

1 How sweet retirement to the Soul,
That loves to be with God,
The happiest moments I have known,
Have been beneath the Shade.

2 Nature this morning, dress'd in green
The Spring once more appears,
The birds in homage to their God,
Their warblings have begun.

3 The sun in grandeur makes his way,
And darkness flies before,
Tis Sabbath and my soul will go,
To join the Saints of God.

Submission

1 And am I doomed to feel those woes,
Is this thy will thou Sovereign Lord,
Then let me nothing wish or choose,
But yield submission to thy word.

2 My soul in humble Confidence,
In thee the Author of my bliss:
Looks up and longs for holiness,
And waits to prove its happiness.

3 I would be every moment thine
In every thought and word adore,
To thy unerring will resign
And never Sin against thee more.

4 O thou that knowest my inmost Soul
Grant me the visits of thy face
My every thought and word control
By the sweet power of Sovereign grace.

Mourning

1 Come O my saviour Sweetly Come
Fill all this mighty Void.
Prepare me for my future home
Where Sin is all destroyed.

2 This world no comfort can afford
I long to be above,
Haste then and fill me gracious Lord
with all that weight of love.

3 When will those Scenes of Sorrow end
And give me sweet relief,
And bring me to my heavenly friend
Beyond this world of grief.

Vanity of the World

1 How vain the glittering toys of life,
To souls renew'd by grace divine:
Who, tired of noise of Sin and Srife,
On Jesus promises recline.

2 How Short the term of life below,
Evill and few the days of man;
But that bright world to which we go,
None but immortal minds can Scan,

3 Bright Scenes of Glory there prepared
For all who love religion here,
Those who in pains of life have shared
Shall in that world of Joy appear.

Religion a balm

1 Rouse then my Soul rise up and fly:
This world can give the *(thee)* no relief.
Religion, of all below the sky;
Alone can cure thy Soul of grief.

2 Nothing below can Sooth thy woes.
The joys of earth are all but Vain:
Time only Shows thee as it flies*("flies" scratched through)* goes
This world is Vanity and lies, *(entire line scratched through)*
How false and fading is thy gain.

3 But heaven invites to real Joys,
Sublime, eternal and divine,
Which sin nor pain can nee'r annoy,
But Crowns and Glory Shall be thine.

On Solitude

1 Solitude: how lovely and how sweet,
How dear the silence of this calm retreat.
Here precious truth, the good which I pursue
Gives all her shining beauty to my View.

2 Solitude, Thy Simple Silence will display,
The powers of truth and charm my fears away
That truth which millions proudly dare to Slight
O truth my treasure and supreme delight.

3 Solitude: sweet scene of contemplative light.
Where nought but truth can reign amid the night
Truth undissembled points my onward course,
To Joys immortal, To God the glorious Source.

4 Solitude forsaken by the rich and great.
The wicked fly thee, and thy secrets hate.
To me thou art the Channell of Sweet union.
And the great mean of heavenly communion

5 Solitude: how oft thy Shade has been the place
Where my redeemer hath unveiled his face.
Or grove, or cottage or in field or wood,
It matters not thy Silence Still is good.

6 Solitude: how precious is thy Silence now.
From noise and Strife, from vanity and Show,
I fly to hide me, in thy Silent Shade,
Converse with God, and be more humble made.

O the Lords day

1 This is the day of God, when thousands go
Up to his house to worship him below.
Gladly my soul shall join the happy band
And sing with those that round his Altar stand.

2 Today in sweetest harmony they join,
And loudest anthems sing in songs divine,
Angells above and Saints below unite,
To adore that God who dwells in endless light.

3 Tis God's own day appointed by his love,
That men may raise their grateful hearts above

A day of rest from labour and from care
Mortalls your hearts and voices now prepare

4 This day declares a soverein *(sovereign)* God in heaven
And men on earth approve his mercy given
In Zions courts the crowding saints adore
And loudest Anthems Sing forevermore

5 My Soul will go, and meet the holy choir
Nor will I stay in Sin or back retire,
My Voice Shall Join in Songs of praise and love
The holy saints that worship him above.

6 From worldly Care and buisness now Set free
I will employ my moments Lord with thee
No jarring note shall in my song be found
But sweetest melody be heard around.

On a Wheel

1 Lucy, while round your wheel you Send
Pray take the hints twas form'd to lend
An emblem of your life tis found
While thus you turn it round and round.

2 Since all your years that roll away,
Are but Small Circles of a day.
Your distant good you still pursue,
And every day, your toil renew.

3 As you each night look for your rest:
And gladly leave your wheel uncas'd
And when your daily task is done:
And you your even thread have spun,

4 So let your life like even twine,
And like a smooth well finished line
But not a foul or tangled clue,
Nor yet a thread oft snapt in two,

5 So shall a full reward be Sure.
A rest that ever will endure,
A rest of happiness refined
A bliss of body and of mind.

On Man

1 Man: was first formed of hardy mould
Patient in trouble brave and bold,
Braving all dangers bearing toil,
To Sail the Seas or plow the Soil.

2 Man: Seeks the good that barning yeilds *(yields)*
Or follows glory in the fields:
Yet though all those gifts possess;
Without a woman is unblest.

3 Man: never was in Joy Complete
Till woman came as a help meet,
Women from man protection find,
Man may by woman be refined.

4 Woman: must sooth the mental strife
And Sweeten all the Ills of life
Let each enchanting pleasing grace
Adorn the beauties of her face.

5 Woman is lovely when retired,
And only then is most admired,

While in her mild domestick Sphere,
Tis then with grace her charms appear.

6 Woman that would be learned or great
Seeks what is foreign to her State.
She ought to know each winning way
And rule: by Seeming to obey.

On the Morning

1 Behold, the rosy mornings dawn
While Sweetly blushing o'er the lawn
The Clouds reflect a radiant Stream
And dew drops tip the mountain brim.

2 The busy bees their Toil renew
Buzz thro the field and Sip the dew
But yonder comes the God of day
With Splendour gilds the ethereal way.

3 The groves rejoice the birds now sing
And make the Shady Valies *(valleys?)* ring.
Wake'd, by the Suns prolific ray
Nature in Verdure now looks gay.

4 The roses bloom the plants revive,
The groves again begin to live,
While Streams attentive to the sound,
Burst from the earth, and dance around.

5 The ploughman now new Shapes his mould
The yeilding earth as farm'd of Old,
Produces plenty; every field,
A golden harvest soon will yield.

6 The farmers heart with raptures glows
While in his barns his fruits he Stows,
Gratefull in praises to his God,
He turns his Course and homeward plods.

Rural Scenes

1 To rural Scenes ye muses guide,
Where nature wantons in her pride
On mossy banks, where opening flowers
Form pleasant aramathian bowers.

2 Lead me to founts and limpid rills,
To vales and lawns and Sunny Hills:
Where trees exclude the noon tide ray,
And sweet refreshing Zephyrs play.

3 There from the fetters of the great,
Triumphant piles and rooms of State,
Not plagued by sycophantic knaves
Illustrious Villians fawning Slaves.

4 I'd live retired and serene,
Forgot unenvied and unseen,
Yet not a hermitage I'd choose
Nor would I live a true recluse.

5 But with a friend unbend the Soul
In social converse: And controul,
My passions when they would rebell,
By prayer and praise within my Cell.

6 Removed from discord and from Strife
Serene, go down the Stream of life.

While oft beneath the Spreading Shade,
Where fountains murmur thro the glade.

7 Else, in a grot perfumed with flowers,
In harmless mirth I'll spend my hours,
Or gravely talk, or sweetly Sing,
My friend shall strike the trembling string.

On Judgement

1 Judgement: with what an awful pomp twill burst
At midnight, to give more dread to this dread Scene,
From tenfold darkness, when awakened first,
Those who an age, have in their Silence been.

2 Judgement: how awful to the waking world
Who long have slumber'd in the silent tombs
Nature now Strugling will at once be hurld
In strong Convulsions to her native womb.

3 Judgement: great day for which all time was made
Day of decision and of dread despair,
At thought of thee all earthly grandeurs fade
Dignities and crowns and honours quake and fear.

4 Judgement: that dread tribunal where our doom
By conscience now foretold will prove it true
At once each Sublunary wish gives room
And hope Still grasps the prospect that is new.

5 Judgement: how welcome to the happy few
Who owned their God on earth and ever love
To walk in Virtues ways and to renew
Each day their covenant to be more above.

6 Judgement: the terror of the wicked band
Who live in vain amusement here below
When God on high Shall lift his awful hand
And deal to Sinners a tremendous blow.

On Happiness

1 O hapiness: our beings end and aim.
Whatever earthly good may be thy name,
That Sent Something which provokes a sigh:
For which we dare either to *(live?)* or die.

2 Happiness: thou near us yet beyond us lies,
O'er looked seen double by the weak and wise
A plant of heaven yet often sought below
Say in what Soil here dost thou deign to grow.

3 Happiness where grows it, and if vain our toil
Justly we blame the Culture, not the Soil.
Confined nowhere, can it yet be sincere.
Tis no where to be found; or everywhere.

4 Happiness: tis heavens firm law Confest
That man Should Seek it, and obtain a rest.
Some are, and will be rich, but not from hence
Is happiness derived; nor yet from Sense.

5 Happiness: from heaven alone can man possess
From gods free bounty, this treasure all confess
Condition, circumstance is not the thing,
The Peasant may be happy, as the King.

6 Happiness: when real proves a real friend
And will from every Ill our Souls defend

Tis God within us, this alone give
Courage to die: or fortitude to live.

The Choice

1 Let heroes seek renown in arms,
And rush to noise in warm alarms,
To Shining palaces resort,
And dunces Cringe and bow at Court.

2 Mine be the Scenes of rural life,
Distant from noise, remote from Strife:
From the Belle, or the Beau,
The lawless (?) dance or midnight Show.

3 Deep in the centre of a grove,
By nature form'd for silent love:
Whose banks adorned with opening flowers
Perfume the landscapes, roseate bowers.

4 Here my lone mansion, will I raise,
Unlike the domes of modern days
Devoid of pomp, with plainness form'd
With reeds and glossy Shells adorned

5 No costly boards shall grace my hall
But vines ascend against the wall,
Their branches shall together twine:
Their Clusters will afford me wine.

6 Down from the rack a limpid rill:
Shall give me drink, and sweet distill
Around my house shall Cedar grow
Extended in a Shady grove.

7 High in the air Shall poplars rise,
And Shoot their heads towards the skies
Whereon the birds their nests may form
Securely Shelter'd from the storm.

Death a boon

1 Think, mortals what favours you enjoy
Nor believe that your en(d) is too Soon
What wills your lives here annoy
To die then is mans greatest boon.

2 Think: what Strange fondness for life,
To be thus enamoured with harm
What a world of Contention and Strife
And yet it has power to Charm.

3 Think: whence this strange magic power
Why should we fear death as a foe,
Or why do we recoil from this hour:
And covet to linger in woe.

4 Think: men of Conscience how oft,
Your sad tale of guilt you renew;
The voice that sometimes is soft,
When a full dread of death will ensue.

5 Think: mortals how you wish to be spared
While you mourn your quick fleeting breath
Every evill is light when compared,
To the dire approaches of death.

6 Think of judgement, Ah: there is the fear,
That prompts you to wish a long stay,

Your account has been long in Arrears,
And you know you have nothing to pay.

7 Think. on Christ, and your debt shall be paid
For his death your Salvation ensures,
Remember the grave where your Savior was laid
And Calmly descend into yours.

Content

1 And Shall I murmur at my lott.
My Soul now Shudders at the thought
I bid the pomp of earth Adieu,
I have no memory now for you.

2 If I feel misery, I'll adore.
My gracious Soverign Still the more:
His love Shall be my only pride,
And I will nothin(g) prize beside.

3 In thee is wealth comfort and might
My wandrings prove thee infinite
All that I have I give to thee
And pray that I may holy be.

4 I feel my weakness and deplore
A heart that will not love thee more
The more I love the more I prove,
My Soul is base and slow to love.

5 O Jesus bid me quickly rise
And soar above this earth and Skies,
till by thy mercy, I am toss'd
Into that Sea of love, and lost.

The Grove

1 Ye songsters of this peaceful Grove,
Who loudly Sing your makers praise
No more in quest of men I rove,
For all have wandered from his ways.

2 Tis God who props my Sinking Soul
And Sets me free from all below,
Should I traverse from pole to pole,
Where Could I better pay my Vow.

3 O I can dwell with man no more,
Your gentle warbling suits me best,
Life's fond delusions I give o'er
For all its pleasures are a Jest.

4 O Could I love him as I ought,
And tune to him my ceaseless Voice,
His love exceeds all human thought,
And makes the wondering Soul rejoice.

5 Had I a thousand humble hearts,
My Saviour they should all be thine
If thou approve: thy Smile impart,
A light that nothing can outshine.

Religion

1 Religion: gives a peace of Soul
The world can never know
It guides us to that heavenly goal
And weans from all below.

102

2 Religion: Ofspring *(offspring)* of the skies,
Calms all our troubles here,
And by its Strength the Sinner flies
To Joys that are Sincere.

3 Religion: bids our Sorrows Cease
By faith we mount above,
And find in Christ a sweet release
And know his pardoning love.

4 Religion: weans us from the toys
And trifles of this life.
It makes us seek for real Joys,
Secure from noise and Strife.

5 Religion: fits us for our home,
And guides us on our way.
We look for happiness to come
In Scenes of endless Day.

On Love

1 Love: O how charming is the Sound,
To Saints who long for heaven,
It cheers the Soul and cures the wound
That vanity has given.

2 Love: melts the heart and lifts the mind,
From every earthly Joy:
Makes all its jarring Strings combine,
In his divine employ.

3 Love: cures the deepest wounds of heart
That Sin and Sorrow give.

And will temptations direst Smart,
In Softest words relieve.

4 Love: fills the Soul with heavenly life,
And Cheers the drooping Saint.
It puts an end to war and strife
And stills each sad complaint.

5 Love: fitts the soul to live above,
It turns our hell to heaven:
O for the power of sovereign love,
To dying Sinners given.

Retirement

1 Let me live in that Valley, overshaded with trees
Among rocks, which the Ivy and briars infold
Such Scenes which the world with astonishment see,
Do I with the Joys of rapture behold.

2 Though awfully Silent and naturally rude
I am pleas'd with the peace and the charms they afford
These shades are a temple, where none dare intrude
The lovely abode of my glorious Lord.

3 I am Sick of the Splendours and noise of the day
I will hither retire from thy Sinful Streams
While I contemplate a more glorious display
In the fullest enjoyment of still brighter beams.

4 Ye forests that yeild me such pleasg *(pleasing)* repose
Where Silence and Solitude awfully reign
To you I can boldly each Sorrow disclose
And tell all my pains and freely complain.

The Forest

1 Here I forget and am by all forgot.
Charm'd by the songs of yonder warbling throng
These birds and Streams lend me a pleasing note
To aid my meditation and my Song.

2 Wandering in Scenes peculiar to the night
I'm lost in raptures, and quite worn away
Often the Sun has Spent his morning light
Before I wake to find it open day.

3 Tis here while mantled In the darkest sphere
I can my Sorrows Safely o'er rehearse,
The darkest hours to me are truly dear
(For) here I find the last sweet as the first.

4 There with the beasts so wild I will agree
Mortals alone, my Soul is led to fear,
I feel a natural right Still to be free
Which men deny but no one doubts it here.

On Man

1 Man, always frail, thy glass is run,
Thy barge is toss'd on times rough wave.
How soon thy rambling journey's done
And death conveys thee to thy grave.

2 Man: ever feeble now more frail,
Thy life curtailed of many years,
If famine Come, or plague prevail,
Or death in any Shape appears.

3 Man: as the bay tree fresh and green,
With rich and gaudy trappings on,
Now gay and thoughtless have I seen,
Tomorrow Came and they were gone.

4 Man: read now this Solemn truth
Let it with care your mind engage,
A worm is in the bud of youth,
An(d) eats away the root of Age.

5 Man: though humble be thy lott,
And feeble be thy early Strain,
This truth Should never be forgot,
The pleasure(s) of this world are Vain.

On Friendship

1 Friendship: the sweetest mental grace
How oft profest, by minds too base,
To have thee in possession:
How few will act the noble part
And show that Charity of heart,
Which marks thy true discretion.

2 Friendship: the brightest Gem we find
That brightens in a human mind,
And calls for imitation;
True, many others do the same,
And adds a lustre to thy flame,
Thou brightest Constellation.

3 Friendship: how many loud pretend,
Thy virtues that compose thy name
A real and a sound one,

But yet how oft they will deceive,
When thou art ready to believe,
How quick he proves a false one.

Death a Joy to the Saint

1 Death, most delightfull hour to man,
If dead to all below,
How frail his State how Short the Span
How full of pain and woe.

2 Worlds could not tempt the Saint to tread
Again life's dreary waste,
To view again his day O'er Spread,
With all the gloomy past.

3 His home he sees safe in the Skies,
He bids this world adieu,
While Heaven unfolding to his eyes,
Earth lessens in his View.

4 His Soul, of Jesus full possess'd
By faith's supporting rod.
He sweetly passes to his rest,
The bosom of his God.

5 But oh, of many men: how few,
Are seen on Virtue's Side:
Who day by day their lives review
And nothing seek beside.

6 His joys be mine my reader cries
When my last hour arrives

They Shall be yours my Lord replies
If holy be your lives.

(In a duplication of this verse on another page,
the word Jesus is substituted for the words my Lord).

The Swallow

1 I would learn from the swallow:
Who seldom in flight,
Does she deign to look down,
Or on earth to alight,
from this let me gain
A sweet lesson of love,
For She dwells in the Skies
She is ever above.

2 Tis said on the wing
She takes her repose,
Nor is it on earth
That her Sustenance grows,
Suspended on high,
In the regions of air,
She gathers her food
Tis ethereal fare.

3 She comes with the Spring: all the summer she Stays
And closely she follows: the Suns brighter rays
Like her I would follow: my heavenly Sun,
And the place where he shines: to it would I run.

4 My light shall be love: my food praise and prayer
The fruit of the world: is beset with a Snare.

Tis dangerous food: that we find upon earth
In itself it is hurtful: and more Vile in its birth.

5 The Swallow tis Seldom: She Settles below,
Were it not for her brood, She would never bestow
A thought upon any thing, filthly as dung,
But she must stoop in building: a nest for her young.

6 Let me leave it my Soul: tis a sinful abode:
I will fly from the winter and follow the road
That leads to the mansions of infinite love,
And rest from all labour in regions above.

School Account Book

In the years 1801 and 1802, John Andrew kept an account of the money due him for teaching school. Names of parents, the number of scholars taught, and the amount the family owed him for these two years has survived:

School for 1801   Due Me 1st January

(Parent's name)	Scholars	Dollars
Hezekiah Gray	2 & ½	20 pd.
Betsy Mathews	2	16
Joseph Brawner	1	8
Andrew West	1	8
Shelton White	2	16
Simeon Glenn	2	16
Claborn Webb	3	24 pd.
James Oliver	1	8
William Gooldsby	1	8
Henry Brawner	1	8

Total $132

1802   Due By Me To Sundries 1st January

Hezekiah Gray	9
Ditto	
Clabourn Webb	
John Speer	6
Jack ?coy (McCoy?)	
Oliver	

Family Letters

Many of the following letters are found in G.G. Smith's, *The Life and Letters of James O. Andrew,* Southern Methodist Publishing House, Nashville, 1883, pp. 19-21, 49-54, 186-189.

1. 12-9-1789 from Daniel Grant to Polly Cosby

Sister Polly Cosby:

I use this friendly term from no other motive than this. As you have and expect still to make choice of the mode of worship which I myself have chosen (I hope after mature deliberation), as also I trust you have and do experience in your soul that love of Christ, his ways and people, which hope I have myself in some degree felt, and still, which I think unites my soul to all the people of God of whatever name.

I hear a report hath prevailed about Broad River, that I was about to leave the Methodists and join the Baptists, but it affords me no concern any farther than for the sake of others, but be assured there is nothing to it. I believe there are many good people among them that I highly esteem, but I think their doctrines and opinions have a dangerous tendency.

I was for many years a member of the Presbyterian Church, and love and honor many of them, for though they hold the same opinions for the most part with the Baptist yet they don't abuse them so much, and as I have been for several years well acquainted with Presbyterians, Baptists, and Methodists I am in some measure the more capable to judge for myself.

The Methodists, I know, are a people that are sat at naught by many, but for my part I hope to live and die in fellowship with them. Class Meetings are the ridicule of many, but I think it is the most blessed means to keep up the life of religion in the soul almost of any other, and I don't doubt you have often been greatly blessed at such times, notwithstanding all Satan, the world, and our backwardness can say against it.

I have been truly sensible of the many trials and difficulties yourself and sisters have had to encounter since you have sat out in the service of God; but fear not, greater is he that is in you, than he that is against you; take notice of this precious word, *Be faithful,* and all these things I hope will in the end work for your good. When you are by grace enabled to surmount them you will then be better able to see and shun the devices of Satan.

Aim at more holiness of heart and life, and let all your friends and those around you see by your heavenly life and conversation what you profess to be, viz., a follower of the meek and lowly Jesus.

I was glad to hear you have escaped the snare, so artfully laid for you, and which I hope in God will prove a blessing; bear up under all the difficulties you have to bear, and the greater will be your reward in Heaven, and live near to the Lord, look continually to him and he will support you if you faint not.

Encourage your Sisters in the good ways of God. You have, I expect, all been happily united, and I hope will remain so. Tell them from me that this world has no pleasure compared with that of serving and pleasing God. We shall all soon die, and our business is to endeavor to escape the death that never dies, and so obtain a fitness for that blessed world above where all our sorrows end and everlasting joy takes place, and, while we live here, to live to the glory of our gracious God, recommend him to others, and enjoy his blessed presence and the light of his reconciled countenance, which is better than life, and that this may be your and your Sisters' and my own happy case, let us all earnestly strive, relying for assistance on his almighty arm. Adieu, my friend, live in love and peace, and the God of all Grace enable you so to do.

Daniel Grant

2. 2-16-1813 from John Andrew to son James Osgood Andrew

My Beloved Son

Since I wrote the one you will hereafter receive from Augusta, I received your thrice-welcomed letter. I say thrice for three reasons – I rejoice at it, first, to hear from you and find you are well; secondly because it appears to give satisfaction to your friends here (for it has gone the rounds of your friends) and last of all because it tells that you are engaged in that most important work, and have received the gracious work of GOD in your soul! Oh, my dear boy, your faithfulness proves my life, my joy

Your conflicts, I expect, are many, but they are momentary, and victory is sure if you apply for help and remember you can only conquer through grace. I think the life of an Itinerant Preacher the nearest Heaven of any man on earth. Where he is faithful, divested of every worldly care, secluded from the noise and bustle of the world, and shut up in God, his contemplations are delightful, his engagements in duty pleasant, his life exemplary, and his end glorious.

I am truly glad you have seen your colleague, and more so that you are pleased with him. Strive, my son, to deserve his affection, and if you are united you may improve by his piety and instruction, and nothing will be able to stand against your united zeal; even the tall sons of Anak must give way, and GOD will give you good and great times. Need I say I pray for you and him and your circuit. My manner is to remember you every night in family prayer, and to meet you every evening in private.

I received your letter on Saturday at meeting, and showed it to your Father Marks. He rejoiced to hear from you, and desires me to remember him to you, and to tell you to write him often, for he cannot write. Brother Gray promised me to write you from Augusta. I wrote by him to the care of Brother Lucius; I expect this will be the best way for me to write to you. I don't like to put you to so much expense by mail.

I will not give you the news of the place. Your friend John Webb lies very ill. James Gray is yet single. I expect to teach this year at the old school-house. Brother Robbins' money I expect to get settled, but should I fail I will write to you and you must try and lay it up. Brother Brewer is very low; he can't live long, I think. The society here are still dull. GOD grant a revival. When you write again say something to Nelson and Eady, they desire to be remembered to you. According to your request we have often kissed dear little Harbert, and now ask him what brother said, and his reply is *Kiss me.* Lucy, Betsy, Caroline, Patsy, and little Judy, say love to Brother. I must now give you a few directions, my son. Write more and with greater industry to improve. Take pains in folding and directing. Suppose you keep a journal, it would give me pleasure to peruse it. Write smaller.

Once more and I have done for this time: my sincere wish is to hear of your prosperity. Indeed, I long to see you, but I know it cannot now be. True, I am poor, my son, in the world, but yet I am rich while God is mine and I am his, and in having a son in the Vineyard of GOD. I feel my heart more in the work of God than I have for many years. Your mother is poorly, but I hope she is mending. Farewell, my son; may GOD bless you and keep you. Your mother joins me in love to you, and may Heaven keep you.

Your affectionate Father,
John Andrew

3. Elbert, 7-3-1813   from John Andrew to son, James Osgood
Andrew

My Dear James:

I fear my writing so often may occasion too much expense,
but several occurrences since our last, together with our constant
wishes to give you every caution we think necessary, urge me to
write this. I received yours by Brother Myers, but I have written
you since the one you mention the receipt of.

We are anxious to hear from you, for in your last you say
nothing of your health, and Brother Myers gave us as little
satisfaction. But my sure trust is in GOD that he will preserve
you safe. Oh, my son, we live if you stand fast. While I write
George and Matilda are come. We have had good times here lately.
Merriwether Marks" wife, Patsy Moore, and Theresa Posey have
all been converted and joined society. My Lucy has joined, and I
hope she is in earnest. At our quarterly meeting we had great
times. Many of the young people were brought to weep --Lanier,
Simeon Rogers, Oliver and others. Glory to God, forever and
ever. Doctor Brewer is very near his last hour. Your friends have
all seen your letters, and they wish for your success. Samuel
Leseur is not turned out; I wish he may do better. Your father
Marks told me to say, he thanked you for your letter and intended
to write you. James, have you wrote to Patsy Harvey (his aunt)?
She has been long confined in a melancholy manner. I have
mentioned all that is new.

My son, if you get sick stay not below. Come home till
you recover; and now, my dear boy, may heaven bless you and
direct you. Write me as soon as you get this. Tell me from your
sister and family. Your mother, Matilda, George, and all the family
join me in love to you. Farewell.

Your affectionate Father,
John Andrew

4. letter without date from James Osgood Andrew to his parents

My Dear Parents:

I am yet alive, through the abundant mercy of God, and trying, in my feeble manner, to love God and preach to dying sinners with too little success. I calculate that you are by this time beginning to grow uneasy at not hearing from me for such a length of time, but various circumstances have made it impossible for me to visit the post-office, and have prevented my writing sooner. I also know the expense of postage must be a considerable inconvenience to you. I feel as much bound to serve the Lord as ever, but oh! it seems to me that of all I am of God's servants the most unprofitable. I am, I think, unfaithful, in some degree, in almost everything I undertake. I possess too little of the mind that was in Jesus Christ my Lord. I love God too little; I feel too little for the welfare of Zion's cause. In fact it appears to me that I am lacking in every Christian grace. I want faith, I want love, I want humility. Oh, pray for me that I may obtain all these things. Times in the circuit are not very encouraging, though we have some good times.

Political affairs intefere much with religion. I rejoice to hear of the prosperity of Zion in my dear old society. I often pray for them and long to see them and you. I calculate, the Lord willing, to be at home about Christmas. Our last Q.M. will be held the 13th and 14th of next month. The country has been very sickly, but God has been my protector. I heard from my sister in September, when they were tolerable. I visited them in July; I also visited Mrs. Lambright, who sends a great deal of howdy to you. I will now give you the good news of this place. Commodore Perry has captured the Lake Erie fleet. It is said, I believe from good authority, that Chancey has taken five British vessels; also that our armies have formed a junction and captured the whole of Proctor's army, except himself and his aids, who gallantly took to their heels and left their brethren in arms to shift for themselves.

The consequence of these successes is that a smile of joy rests on the countenance of every honest Republican. Thank God for all his goodness. It will not be worth while to write again. I must conclude by begging to be remembered to all inquiring friends.

I am your dutiful Son,

James O. Andrew

5. 3-11-1818, Wilmington NC from James Osgood Andrew to John Andrew, Lexington, Georgia. (The original of this letter is in SpCl Woodruff, Emory University).

My Dear Father.

Through divine goodness I still live and both myself and family enjoy a reasonable portion of health after leaving your house; my horse recovered of his lameness in a great degree so that I prosecuted my journey in safety. I arrived there on Saturday night and found my family and friends all well. We left Charleston on Tuesday morning following, and after a most fatiguing journey by land we arrived safely in this place the 28th of February, and met with a very warm and affectionate Reception from the people here. O that our coming here may be for good – as it respects religious prospects here I wish I could give a more flattering account at present I can only say our congregations are very large, and appear to be serious O that they may be doers as well as hearers of the word as it is usually the case after considerable ingatherings. I expect there will be considerable outgoing this year. Lord give me wisdom to use the pruning Knife aright. I yet feel like living and dying. A Methodist Preacher *(faded)* my god and feel a continual longing of Soul to be conformed to my Saviors Image. I long most ardently to be an able and successful minister of the New Testament, I trust that these lines will find yourself and family in good health. Give love to my mother and all the girls in short to all my sisters and brothers.

Amelia sends her love to you and I shall expect to receive a letter from you shortly. I am yours in love.

James O. Andrew

P.S. tell Mama that Elizabeth begins to talk but she is getting to be quite a bad child.

6. Mt. Zion, GA, 3-13-1828 from John Andrew to son James Osgood Andrew

My Dear Son,

We received your welcome letter from Conference, and yet you owe us two more, which I expect you never intended to pay. I am glad to hear of the good results of the Conference, and look forward to the success of the Gospel this year without doubt, and with pleasing anticipation. Now, my son, I rejoice in having preachers sent us, yet I wished to have had Brother Wightman; but God's will be done! Another great desire and expectation was to have you near us, a blessing the Conference has never granted us, and I feel I had a right to expect and wish it. If I knew certainly it was the will of my Divine Master to keep you in that station, I would most cheerfully submit, but I do think sometimes that some appointments are not ordered of God. In this instance of your appointment to Charleston I can't see clearly the propriety or the benefit. I fear it has been done to keep you engaged in that controversy with a certain somebody – I don't know who – and I don't like your being concerned in the crooked affair; persecution, or lies, or whatever it may be termed can never hurt the Methodist cause, if we are faithfully engaged, and all that you can write will never convince those who are predetermined to continue in their own opinions. Bishop Soule's sermon speaks for itself; they never can destroy the truths contained therein. 'Tis a sense of those truths, all-important, that rouses their thunders. Why, I have long known that to preach holiness and to urge the necessity of it is to insult the Calvinist, rouse the devil, and create enemies by the numbers. 'Tis true I may not understand the matter rightly, but I do think we should be very cautious how we concern ourselves with these controversial subjects; at any rate I wish you to be little engaged in such. I confess I am liable to err, and I know I would not for thousands of worlds injure that sacred cause. I wish to say nothing that will influence your conduct in any way that is wrong; but, my dear James, we feel tenderly for your reputation as a minister, as a Christian, and as a child; however, then, you may smile at our fears, remember 'tis possible you may be wrong. I have done. Only one expression more: if you continue in the war, be mild, avoid reproachful expressions toward your adversary. Do not wound your enemy by harshness or severity, but ever show the meekness of the Lamb, trying to convince rather than to beat down. I said *we feel*, because your mother makes the same request of you.

My son, I am now done with those (to me) disagreeable matters. Your tender mother says you must write to us before you go to Conference, and tell our dear Amelia she must write as soon as you write to her from Conference. So must Elizabeth write to us. We have enjoyed good health as a family, and have been much blessed. I am now, as I generally am, neither sick nor entirely well, but I feel thankful for my religious enjoyment. God is near to me. I am waiting, expecting my change to come. I commonly enjoy tolerable health. Your dear mother has had some small attacks, but not severe. She now enjoys health. The children are, I believe, all well. In society we are still dull, yet we have had some additions. Remember us to our Amelia, and the children, and to every friend of ours or yours. All join me in love to you all. Adieu! I am in affection,

Sincerely yours,
John Andrew

7. Charleston, 4-11-1828   from James Osgood Andrew to
John Andrew

My Dear Father:

   Your affectionate epistle was received a few days since,
and I was greatly rejoiced to hear of your health, and the peace
and comfort with which the Lord favors you. It would afford me
unspeakable pleasure to surround your table with my wife and
little ones once more, and I still look forward to the time when I
shall enjoy that satisfaction. In reference to your remarks about
my appointment in connection with the Charleston controversy, I
have only to say that neither the appointment nor a participation
in the controversy were sought by me, and I believe that whatever
I may have contributed toward carrying on the quarrel has been
in strict accordance with the character of the Gospel. I shall
endeavor not to sink the character of the minister in the work of
the controversy. Still continue to pray for me that I may be kept
from evil. Since my return from Conference I have had some
reason to believe that God has sent me here. The Church is in a
comfortable state. Little more than a week since we held one of
the greatest camp-meetings ever seen in this neighborhood.
Twenty persons joined at our last love-feast. The meeting was
just noisy enough to have suited you, and I am sure if you had
been there you would have seen that Charleston people were not
afraid of noise. My dear Amelia's health has not been good for
some time past, but she is a little improved within a few days.
Elizabeth, Sarah, and Henrietta go to school and all learn finely.
Henrietta and Sarah both can read, and Elizabeth learns her
grammar, geography, and French pretty well. Little Ann Amelia
is fat and hearty, except a bad cough, which makes her rather
fretful. On Monday morning we expected to sail for New York
on board the ship Saluda, Captain Jennings, the following brethren
accompanying, viz.: L. Pierce, W. Capers, H. Bass, G. Hill, E.
Sinclair, William E. Kennedy, and R. Adams. We shall go to

New York, thence by the way of Albany and Lake Erie to Pittsburgh. Pray for us. Amelia and all unite in love to you. I am in haste and must conclude. You shall hear from me again in Pittsburgh, God willing. My love to all, and believe me,

Yours affectionately,

James O. Andrew

8.   10-25-1828 from Amelia Andrew, Charleston, SC, to her mother-in-law, Mrs. Mary O. Andrew, Watkinsville, Clarke County, Georgia. (The original of this letter is in SpCl, Woodruff Library, Emory University).

I trust my Beloved Mother that this will find you all in the enjoyment of health and happiness. Fathers last was received with much pleasure   we rejoice in that measure of health which as a family you have enjoyed this year   as to ourselves we have abundant cause for gratitude to GOD our mercies have been many and although we have not been altogether free from the chastening hand of affliction yet we know the hand that sent it knew just how much to inflict – and here my Dear Mother I must pause to drop a tear to the memory of that lovely little one, which less than six months ago I fondly called mine. She was indeed lovely and beloved by all that had any knowledge of her   too precious for this world of sin and sorrow. She has been transplanted in a kind soil. I try to submit but sometimes it is hard to say "thy will be done." — as *(faded)* we have been scourged by the Almighty *(2 words faded)* taken from us one whose life was a comment on the doctrines he preached – we may come as near applying this character to Br. Morgan as to any one I know – that as his divine Master he was "holy, harmless, undefiled, separate from sinners." He died of the 'strangers' or yellow fever, that awful disease did not prevail to any great extent this season, but was almost universally fatal from what cause we are unable to determine but Physicians suppose it was in consequence of the remains of the Dengue *(?)* fever in the system, for I do not suppose that more than one hundred of our entire population escaped that to many infirm and aged persons it proved fatal, but in general it was not considered dangerous, though it has left in all — most all who were in any degree debilitated or infirm rheumatic affections of the joints & limbs.

Our dear Brother Morgan appeared to enjoy better health this year than he had done for many years past & was more deeply engaged in the work of God than I ever saw him before the last Sabbath he preached was a day of great labour in consequence of *(3 words faded)***(unk.)** Sabbath for the blacks, *(faded section)* day unusually drawn out & preached *(faded)* his farewell charge, that it was remarked by several that he preached as if he was going away. the next day he was taken sick and after seven days of extreme suffering, he left this for a better world. Mr. Andrew scarcely ever left him & though he could not often speak of his feelings, yet during his sickness, he expressed himself satisfactorily to Mr. Andrews, for the last three or four days he did not appear sensible, except at very short intervals & could not speak much but we needed no dying words to convince us of his fitness for heaven, his life supplied us with every assurance necessary. he has left a heart-broken widow and three small children –the youngest just three weeks old when he died – in consequence of the death of Br. Morgan the labours of the two remaining preachers have necessarily increased but they are assisted by an Almighty hand. Br. Capers has not returned yet from England. We begin now to look for him. I feel as if the year was almost gone & a *move* we must make where to. We know not   he's sure to have no choice but just to go where my Dear Husband may be most useful, though at times I feel some degree of uneasiness about it. Mr. Andrews is at this time from home attending the District Conference, he will return in a few days. The children all desire their love to you all likewise *(faded)* &

Miss Selena *(?)*. Remember me affectionately to all the family including our sisters and their families, Br. & S. Greaves & all inquiring friends. *(faded)* let us know in your next something of Br. Olin –the last account we had of him his health was bad and he had gone to Tennessee Mr. Andrew wrote him in June last, but has received no answer, let us know something of our friends, Mr. & Mrs. Stewart. I have no expectation of seeing you this winter unless we are appointed that way. I remain, my Dear Mother, yours affectionately,

Ann Amelia Andrew

Note: Br. Morgan was Asbury Morgan (8-25-1797 – 9-25-1828) who died of "Stranger's Fever" in Charleston, SC. He had the fever earlier in 1825 and almost died from it. Morgan was appointed to Charleston in 1828.

Family Bible Records

The Andrew Family Bible is located in the Special Collections area of Oxford College, Newton County, GA. It had been donated to the museum at Salem Camp Ground in 1986 by Mrs. Francis Longino of Tampa, Florida. Her husband, Frank Longino, had the book in his possession in the 1960's. When the Bible was donated, the camp ground also possessed Kitty's Cottage, but it, too, has been relocated to Oxford and has been restored behind the Old Church. In that cottage is the spinning wheel of Mary Overton Cosby Andrew. It was given, along with the Bible, to Salem Camp Ground.

While the Bible bears the signature of James Osgood Andrew inside the front cover, it was unmistakably the Bible belonging to his father, John Andrew. The following family information was taken from the Bible and has been placed, along with numerous other family records, on a website of John W. Andrews, a descendant. It is part of the Roots Web's WorldConnect Project. John W. Andrew's genealogical data on the names below may be more accurate in information than the transcription. The transcription lists names of ministers who baptized children and alludes to others with initials and last names, probably midwives. Due to the condition of the material and the cryptic entries and scratch-throughs and over-writes, one needs to view the Bible regarding disputed information or dates.

The Andrew family Bible, a massive New Testament, was printed by T. Allen, Bookseller & Stationer, No. 186, Pearl Street, New York. It is dated 1792.

Page 1

Hardy Harbert Andrew was born 17th March 1811 Babtiz. by Revrd. Lovick Pierce.

William Harvie Andrew born 18th September 1813 baptized by Reverend Hullum: M.W:
    Mrs. Brown

Page 2 - Births

Ann Andrew was born at Waseau (?) SC *21st* of Jan. 1780 babtized by Revd. Mr. Craighead.
    M.W: Mrs. Patton

Mary Burr *(Buer)* Andrew born at Newport 25th October 1786 babtized by Revd. Beverly
    Allen – M.W: Mrs. *(Arnold?)*

Matilda Hull Andrew. born: Washington 21st Septr. 1792 babtized Revd. Arnold M. W:
    Mrs. Hogg.

James Osgood Andrew. born 3rd May, 1794 babtized by Revd. Russell. M.W: *(Stark?)*

Charles Godfrey Andrew. born Long Creek. 10th July 1795 babtized by Revd. Randall and
    Died the 5th October 1796. M.W: Mrs. Hill

Lucy Garland Andrew born Elbert. 25th August 1799. babtized by Revd. Blanton M.W.
    Mrs. Jones

Betsy Sidnor Andrew born Elbert 28th October 1800 Babtized by Revd. Blanton. M. W:
    Dorsey

Scynthia Fletcher Andrew born 1st May 1802 Elbert County babtized by. Rev. Millegan. M.
    W:Mrs. *(Brown?)*

Caroline Wesly Andrew Born 13th August: 1804. Babtized by Revd. Hill M.W: Mrs. Brown

Patsy Evelina Andrew, born 27th December 1806 babtized by Revd. Capell, Elbert County

(this line unreadable save for) Andrew was born

Page 3 - Births

(Note: It appears that this page is a copy-over of the preceding one in better hand).

Hardy Harbert Andrew. Born Elbert County: 17th March 1811 Babtized by Revd. Pierce. M:
    W. Mrs. Goss.

William Harvie Andrew: Born 18th September 1813. Elbert County: Babtized by: Revd.
    Hullum: M.W: Mrs. Brown

We have had no more, that never were named: they died in a few moments of birth:

Elizabeth Mason Andrew. Daughter of James & Amelia Andrew and our g.daughter. Born in
Wilmington, North Carholina: on the 4ᵗʰ of April: 1817: Baptized by Revd. William
M. Kennedy: m.W: Mrs.

Mary Overton: Andrew Daughter of James and Amelia Andrew Born

Frances Mildred Spencer: *(g)*Daughter was born 7ᵗʰ April 1814 *(pos. 1811)*. Baptized by
Revd. Pierce. M:W: Mrs. *Kerlin*: Elbert County

Mary Overton: Spencer Born Elbert County: 11ᵗʰ September, 1814 Babtized by Revd. Bishop
Asbury M:W: Mrs. Brown.

James Andrew: Spencer. Born Oglethorpe County 3ʳᵈ December 1816 Baptized by Revd.
James Smith. M.W: Miss Curry

Overton Fletcher Davenport, Son of William & Betsy Davenport, Born at Oglethorpe County
10ᵗʰ February 1820 MW: Miss Curry.

Lucy

John Andrew Wright son of John and Lucy Wright was born Oct 9ᵗʰ 1831 Clk. Cty. *(?)*

Page 4 - Births

Ann: Daughter of John and Ann Andrew: was born at Wascaw: SC: on the 20th of January
1780: baptized By Reverend Creaghead: M.W. Mrs. Patton.

Mary Burr *(Buer)*: Daughter of John & Mary Buer Andrew. born Newport Georgia on the
25th of October 1786. Babtized by Beverly Allin: M.W. Mrs. Oswald.

James Osgood Andrew: Son of John and Mary: O Andrew: born 3rd May 1794 in Wilkes
County: Georgia: baptized by: Rev. Russell. M.W. Mrs. Starkes.

Matilda: Hull: Andrew born Wilkes County: 25th September 1792. Baptized by Revd.
Arnold. M.W. Mrs. Hogg.

Charles Godfrey Andrew. born Oglethorpe County: on 10th of July 1795 baptized by Revd.
Randle: M.W: Mrs. Hill

Lucy Garland Andrew: born Elbert County: 25th August 1799 Baptized by Revd. Blanton:
M.W. Mrs. Jones.

Betsy Sidnor: Andrew Born: Elbert County, 28th October 1800 Babtized by Revd. Blanton.
M.W. Mrs. Dorsey:

Scynthia Fletcher Andrew: born 1st May 1802: Elbert County:

Babtized by Revd. Millegan
   M.W. Mrs. Dorsey.

Caroline: Wesley: Andrew: Born Elbert County: 13th August 1804
Babtized by Revd. Hill
   M.W. Mrs. Brown.

Patsy: Evelina: Andrew: Born 27th December 1806: Elbert County
Babtized by Revd.
   Capell: M.W. Mrs. Goss.

Judy: Andrew: Harvey: Born Elbert County. 7th February 1809
Babtized by Revd. Ansley:
   M.W. Mrs. Brown.

Page 5 – Marriages

John Andrew. was married to Ann Lambright. 11th Day of February
1779 at the Ervhans:
   South Carolina By Revd. Gormrly.

John Andrew. was married to Mary Burr Andrew 20th September
1785. at Colo.ns Island. By
   Rev. Holmes.

John Andrew Married to Mary: Overton: Cosby in Elbert County.
Georgia on the 11th
   December 1795 by Revd. Richd. Ivey.

James O. Andrew was married to Ann Amelia Mcfarland on the
first Day of May 1816 in
   Charleston: SC By Revd.

Betsy Sidnor Andrew to William Davenport 10th December *(1818)* by Rv. G. Christian,
Oglethorpe.

Ann Andrew, Daughter of John and Ann Andrew was Married the   to Abram I. Roberts at
Coon Sahatchie By Revd.

Lucy G. Wright married to Wm. R. *Henry* Nov. 30 1844 by Rev. John *Simmons.*

Mary: Burr: Andrew Daughter of John and Mary Andrew was married the 2nd of July 1807
To Samuel Lesueur at Elbert County Georgia by Revd. Gabriel Christian.

Matiilda Hull: Andrew Daughter of John & Mary O. Andrew was married to George T.
Spencer: on the 14th day of December 1809 By Revd. Gabriel Christian in Elbert
County: Georgia.

Lucy G. Andrew was married to John Wright Clark County Geo. May 10th 1830

Page 6 – Deaths

Charles: Godfrey: Andrew: Son of John and Mary: Overton. Andrew Died in Oglethorpe
County the 5th October 1796 happy soul fled from woe:

Scynthia: Fletcher: Andrew: Died 5th December 1803. Elbert County: Short was thy passage
to the friendly Tomb: go sweetest Babe: thy master Calls thee.

John Andrew Died in Clark County Geo. March 10th 1830 Aged 72 years and 6 months

funeral by Rev. T. Samford C verses 1st Cor. 15:55-6-7

Judy Harvey Andrew Daughter of John and Mary O. Andrew died in Clark Cty Geo June 23rd 1833 funeral by T. Samford

John W. Andrews' Family Tree

The following information is taken from the website of John W. Andrews, a part of the Roots Web's WorldConnect Project:

Rev. John Andrew, b. 9-14-1758, Midway, Liberty Co., GA; d. 3-10-1830 Clarke (now Oconee) Co. GA; bur. Sep. 1858 *(?)*. Funeral by Rev. T. Samford; son of James Andrew and Esther (Hester) Jones; RS, Battalion & South Carolina Dragoons; Pvt. under Gen. Samuel Elbert, GA Troops; Ensign under Gen. Wade Hampton; 7-15-1784 GA Rev. Land Bounty. Warrant #2797, 287 & ½ a. in Washington Co., GA. "He served in a Georgia unit and then served as a quartermaster under Col. Henry Hampton and Gen. Sumter during 1781. He was in the battles at Briar Creek, Fishing Creek and in many skirmishes."

GA Colonial Deeds, p. 153: John Andrew to Hon. Benjamin Andrew, both of Liberty Co. Deed dated 5-8-1786, conveying lot #4, size 50x70' at the public landing near head of North Newport River, being part of 500 a. tract granted John Graves and deeded by William Graves to James Andrew. p. 154: deed conveying 448 a. in Liberty Co. on which the grantor's father, James Andrew, lived and died. (same parties & date).

m1/ 2-10-1779 in Ervhans, SC by Rev. Gormley, Ann Lambright. Child: Ann Andrew, b. 1-20-1780 in Wascom, SC; m2/ 4-25-1785, Midway, Liberty, Georgia, Site 25 in Colonels Island, Mary Buer (Manoe), b. 1-27-1767, Midway, Liberty, Georgia. Child: Mary Buer Andrew, b. 10-25-1786 in Newport, Liberty County, GA.

m3/ 12-11-1791, Elbert Co., GA, by Rev. Richard Ivey, Mary Overton Cosby, b. ca 1772. Chrn: Matilda Hull, b. 9-25-1792, Wilkes Co., GA; James Osgood, b. 5-3-1794, Wilkes Co.,

GA; Charles Godfrey, b. 7-10-1795, Oglethorpe Co., GA; Martha; Lucy Garland, b. 8-25-1799, Elbert, GA; Elizabeth (Betsy) Sydnor, b. 10-28-1800, Elbert, GA; Scynthia Fletcher, b. 5-1-1802, Elbert, GA; Caroline Wesley, b. 8-13-1804, Elbert, GA; Patsy Evelina, b. 12-27-1806, Midway, Liberty Co., GA; Judy Harvie, b. 2-7-1809, Elbert, GA; Hardy Harbert, b. 3-17-1811, Elbert, GA; William Harvie, b. 9-18-1813, Elbert Co., GA.

Midway Records

In the volume, *History and Published Records of the Midway Congregational Church, Liberty County, Georgia,* published in 1979 was actually the result of a combination of two volumes. The first was *The History of the Midway Congregational Church,* by James Stacy, 1903; and the second was *The Published Records of Midway Church,* compiled by James Stacy in 1894. The following extracts indicate those pages which pertain to the Andrew family:

p. 19   Under the heading, Those Who Followed: Those having families in 1754 are listed. Among the names are included: Josiah Osgood, Rev. John Osgood, Benjamin Andrew. Three of these families, viz. that of John and Sarah Mitchell and Benjamin Andrew, were from Pon Pon.

In 1758, Samuel Jeans and family, James Andrew and family, and (Mrs.) Lydia Saunders.

p. 30   Those signing the articles of church constitution: Josiah Osgood, Sr., Benjamin Andrew, Joseph Andrew, John Andrew.

p. 31   contd. John Osgood, M. Andrews, Josiah Osgood, Jr., John Osgood, Jr.,

p. 96   I first mention Hon. Benjamin Andrew, one of the original colony from Carolina, president of the first Executive Council, convened upon the election of John Adam Treutlin governor of Georgia in 1777, and three years afterwards elected a member of the Continental Congress, of whose home Bartram, in his travels, speaks of as "the seat of virtue, where hospitality, piety, and philosophy formed the happy family, where the weary traveler and stranger found a hearty welcome, and from whence, it must be his own fault, if he departed without being greatly benefited."

He was a man of wealth and influence, having two homes, a summer and a winter, one on the Riceboro road, which he afterwards sold to John Lambert, and one on Colonel's Island. He was associate justice with George Walton for a number of years, also a member of the legislature. In later years he removed to Richmond county and made Augusta his home, and where he died. Mrs. Elizabeth Andrew Hill, of Griffin, GA, and one of the vice-presidents of the "Daughters of the Revolution," is a great granddaughter of his.

p. 143 Rev. John Andrew, son of James and Esther Andrew, original settlers, and members of Midway church, was born in Liberty county September 14, 1758, and baptized October 14th following. His father, James Andrew, was clerk of the Midway church for five years, from 1766 to 1771. His father died December 5, 1770, and his mother July 6, 1773, and he being left, a lad of fifteen years old. The war of the Revolution coming on, he entered the army till its close. The coast being all desolated at the close of the war, he removed to what is now known as Columbia, and where he joined the Methodist church and also entered the ministry of that church. For awhile he located and taught school. He died in 1830, and was buried in Oconee county, about one mile north of Farmington. He was the first native born Methodist minister, of the traveling connection, in the state.

p. 144 Bishop James Osgood Andrew. He always felt an interest in the home of his ancestor. In passing through Liberty county once, he went to the graveyard and knelt near the graves of his grandparents and their pastor, and lifted up his soul in prayer to God.

p. 193   John Andrew signed the will of John Lambert, Liberty County, 9-29-1785.

p. 262-263   Clerks: James Andrew, 1766-1771; Select Men: 1767-69, 1772-78 Benjamin Andrew.

p. 279   Rev. John Osgood married twice, and had two children, Sarah who married John Quarterman, Jr. and Mary who married Joseph Way. His first wife was Hannah ___ and his second wife was Mary Andrew, sister of Judge Benjamin Andrew.

The Andrew family was quite large, as follows: Benjamin, James, the father of John and grandfather of Bishop James Osgood Andrew, Joseph, and Lydia who married first Saunders and second John Winn, Sr.; Hannah who married first George Godfrey and second Rev. John Alexander; Elizabeth, second wife of Richard Baker; and Mary, 2nd wife of Rev. John Osgood.

Published Records:

p. 49   Early settlers arrived from Dorchester and Beach Hill, in South Carolina, to Midway and Newport, in Georgia, for inhabitation: Benjamin Andrew and family, from Pon Pon, May 10, 1754; Josiah Osgood and family, March 31, 1754; Rev. John Osgood and family, June 8, 1754; James Andrew and family, March 13, 1758.

p. 75   Marriages: John Quarterman to Sarah Osgood, Oct. 11, 1754; Richard Baker to Elizabeth Andrew, April 28, 1755; Joseph Way to Mary Osgood, March 12, 1759; John Bacon to Ann Andrew, Feb. 17, 1761; Benjamin Andrew to Mary Philbin, Sept. 28, 1762; Samuel Bacon to Mary Andrew, 1764; John Davis to Rebecca Andrew, February, 1766.

p. 78   Marriages contd.: John Andrew to Manoe Andrew, April 25, 1785.

p. 86   Births: Rebecca, to Joseph and Mary Ann Andrew, March 19, 1748; Mary to Joseph and Mary Ann Andrew, Sept. 8, 1750; John to Benjamin and Elizabeth Andrew, Oct. 2, 1751; Benjamin to Benjamin and Elizabeth Andrew, April 13, 1753; Elizabeth to Benjamin Andrew, Sept. 25, 1755; Susanna to Benjamin Andrew, July 14, 1756.

p. 87   Births contd.: John to James Andrew, Sept. 14, 1758; Hannah to Benjamin Andrew, October 16, 1759; Thomas to James Andrew, July 20, 1760. (**Note:** Thomas must have been an afflicted child).

p. 88   Births contd.: son to Benjamin Andrew, July, 1761; Lydia to Joseph and Mary Andrew, Sept. 28, 1761.

p. 89   Births contd.: Mary to James Andrew, April 14, 1764; Charles to Joseph Andrew, Sept. 28, 1764; Sarah to Benjamin Andrew, Dec. 19, 1764; Mary Buer to Benjamin Andrew, Jan. 27, 1767; Ann to Joseph and Mary Ann Andrew, May 4, 1767.

p. 90   Births contd.: Sanders to Joseph and Mary Ann Andrew, May 3, 1769; Lydia to Benjamin and Mary Andrew, July 11, 1769; Elizabeth to Benjamin and Mary Andrew, Oct. 18, 1771; Son to Joseph and Mary Ann Andrew, Oct. 15, 1771.

p. 110   Baptisms: Elizabeth, dau. of Benjamin Andrew, Oct. 20, 1754; Susanna, dau. of Benjamin Andrew, Aug. 22, 1756; Richard, son of Benjamin Andrew, May 21, 1758.

p. 111   Baptisms contd.: John, son of James Andrew, Oct. 14, 1758; Hannah, dau. of Benjamin Andrew, Nov. 25, 1759; Joseph, son of Joseph Andrew, March 30, 1760; Thomas, son of James Andrew, Aug. 17, 1760.

p. 112 Baptisms contd.: Lydia, dau. of Joseph Andrew, Nov. 13, 1761; Mary, dau. of James Andrew, 1764.

p. 113 Baptisms contd.: Mary Buer, dau. of Benjamin and Mary Andrew, March 1, 1767; Ann, dau. of Joseph and Mary Ann Andrew, June 7, 1767.

p. 114 Baptisms contd.: Sanders, son of Joseph and Mary Andrews, June 18, 1769; Lydia, dau. of Benjamin and Mary Andrew, July 25, 1769; Elizabeth, dau. of Benjamin & Mary Andrew, Nov. 24, 1771; John Osgood, son of Joseph and Mary Ann Andrew, Jan. 12, 1772.

p. 132 Deaths: Elizabeth, dau. of Benjamin Andrew (in Carolina) October or November, 1755; Richard, son of Benjamin Andrew, Sept. 6, 1758; Joseph, son of Joseph Andrew, October 13, 1760; Hannah, dau. of Benjamin Andrew, Oct. 27, 1761; Son of Benjamin Andrew, Oct. 28, 1761; Susannah, w. Benjamin Andrew, 1762.

p. 133 Deaths contd.: Mary, dau. of James & Hester Andrew, Aug. 15, 1765.

p. 134 Deaths contd.: Mary Ann, dau. of Joseph and Mary Ann Andrew, Feb. 13, 1769.

p. 135 Deaths contd.: James Andrew, Dec. 5, 1770; Charles, son of Joseph Andrew, May 18, 1771; Esther, widow of James Andrew, July 6, 1773; Rev. John Osgood, Aug. 2, 1773.

p. 136 Deaths contd.: Joseph Andrew, buried April 11, 1774.

p. 137 Deaths contd.: John, son of Benjamin and Mary Andrew, March 17, 1776; Rebecca, wife of John Davis (dau. of Joseph

Andrew), Dec. 5, 1777; Lydia, wife of John Winn, Sr., May 3, 1778.

p. 138 Deaths contd.: Mary Burr, wife of John Andrew, 1786; Mary, wife of Benjamin Andrew, Jan. 13, 1787.

p. 148 Deaths contd.: Sanders Andrew, October 1808.

Cosby Information

Mary Overton Cosby, wife of John Andrew, was a child of Charles Cosby who lived in Elbert County on Beaverdam Creek. His will is in Elbert Will Bk. B, p. 90 and has been abstracted in the GA DAR Historical Collections, pp. 6-7 (v3, Records of Elbert Co., GA).

The will names wife Elizabeth; g.daughter Lucy Cosby Harvie; g.daughter Elizabeth Sydnor Harvie; g.daughters Matilda Hull Andrew, Lucy Garland Andrew; son Robert Cosby; daughters Patsy Ragland, Barbara Miner Cosby; g.daughter Lucy Hawkins Cosby, daughter of James; sons Richmond, James, David & Charles Scott; slaves Hannibal, Charity, Antony, Lucy, Melinda. A son, probably deceased, Fortunatus, father of Elizabeth Sydnor Cosby.

Will signed: 3-10-1800; recorded 8-2-1802.

In *Spotsylvania County Records, 1721-1800,* by William Armstrong Crozier (Baltimore: Southern Book Company), 1955, pp. 268, 391, 395, the property of Charles Cosby is listed prior to his removal to Georgia.

Deed Abstracts
Relating to John Andrew

Elbert, Bk. D, 1796-1797:

p. 25   21 Dec. 1796, Benjamin Goss, Sr., of Elbert co., GA., farmer, to John Andrew of Oglethorpe Co., GA, for L80 or $400, all the land on which he now lives, 220 acres in Elbert Co. on Cedar Creek, waters of Broad River, adj. Grey, Jesse White, Charles Goss, & James Brown, in fee simple, to have possession 1 Feb. next. (signed) Benjamin Goss. Test: Thos. B. Scott, J.P., Hezekiah Gray. Regd. 21 Dec. 1796.

p. 138 13 Dec. 1797, Benjamin Goss, Sr. & Elizabeth, his wife, to John Andrew, all of Elbert Co., land where Benjamin Goss., Sr. formerly lived, 270 acres on Cedar Creek in sd. co., adj. W. by Jessy Whyte, E. by Hugh McDonald & Charles Goss, N. by Joseph Brawner, S. by Hezekiah Gray & John Webb, including the part of land given formerly verbally by Benjamin Goss, Sr. to Benjamin Goss, Jr., to run in direct line from Gray's corner to Goss's corner, being part of Chandler's survey & other part of tract called Meritt's survey, for $300, in fee simple. (signed) Benjamin Goss. Wit: (torn).

Elbert, Bk. E, 1798-99:

p. 77   Elbert Co., GA: 20 July 1798, Benjamin Baker & Comfort, his wife, being now inhabitants of Franklin Co., GA, to John Andrew of Elbert Co., for $50, Lot No. 7 in Elberton, Elbert Co., adj. Eli Eavinson, Middleton Woods & John W. Whitney, 1 acre, in fee simiple. (signed) Benjamin Baker, Comfort Baker. Wit: John Carrell, J.P. Regd. 20 July 1798.

Wilkes, Bk. RR, 1798-1805:

p. 208 Howell Jarrett, sheriff of Wilkes Co., in virtue of a writ of fi.fa. issued from Inferior Court of Wilkes Co. in judgement obtained by Thomas Fontaine agst. John Andrew. I have levied on the following negroes as property of said Andrew, viz: Bob, Bess, July, Moses, Bob, Joe, & Davy. Advertised & sold at Wilkes Court House, 6 Mar. instant. Thomas Fontaine was the highest bidder, for $725, 14 Mar. 1799. (signed) H. Jarrett, shff. Test. Jno. Foster, Corn., Jno. McLeod, J.P. Rec. 14 Mar. 1799.

Elbert, Bk. F, 1799-1800:

p. 137 Elbert Co., GA: 5 Dec. 1799, John Brawner & Mary, his wife, to John Andrew, all of sd. co., for $214, on Falling Creek waters in sd. co., being where Robins Andrews now lives, sd. to be 123 acres, near the ford, to & down branch to creek, adj. Jarratt, J. Settle (Little?). (signed) John Brawner, Mary Brawner. Test: John Staples, J.P. Regd. 17 Apr. 1800.

Elbert, Bk. G, 1801-02:

p. 34 GA: 30 Jan. 1801, John Andrew of Elbert Co., GA, to George Ward of Newcastle Co., Deleware. Andrew is indebted on bond, 11 Apr. 1799, to Ward, for $3613. Pmt. was supposed to be 1 Sept. 1799, for $1815.50. For $100 & to secure bond, 2 tracts: Cedar Creek in Elbert Co., 300 acres, orig. granted to Joel Chandler, adj. Jesse White, Joe Browner, & Wm. Robins, being plantation where John Andrew now lives. Other tract on

Falling Creek in sd. co., 300 acres with 2 small improvements, orig. granted to Bazill Brawner, adj. Archey Jarratt, Henry Brawner, & William Suttles. If Andrews pays, 1 Jan. 1802, $1815.50 with interest, then this to be void, else to remain in full force. (signed) Jno. Andrew. Wit: Nathl. Cocke, Wm. Pope. Regd. 19 Feb. 1801.

p. 56   Elbert Co., GA: 1 Apr. 1801, John Andrew & Mary Overton, his wife, to Abraham Isaac Roberts, all of sd. co., for $600, on Falling Creek in sd. co. in 2 tracts adj. each other, where Robins Andrews formerly lived, orig. granted to Bazill Brawner, sd. to be 250 acres, adj. E. by Isaac Settles, W. by Jessy Settles & William Settles, Senior, N. by Henry Brawner, S. by Archer Jarratt, in fee simple. (signed) John Andrew, Mary O. Andrew. Wit: Hezekiah Gray, J.P. Regd. 2 Apr. 1801.

p. 136   Elbert Co., GA: 4 Oct. 1800, John Andrew & Mary O., his wife, to James Brown, Sen., all of sd. co., for $900, all tract where sd. Andrew now lives, 260 acres on Cedar Creek in sd. co., adj. Hezekiah Gray, Jesse White, Joseph Brawner, & Silvester Hammonds, on & down creek. (signed) John Andrew, Mary O. Andrew. Wit: A. Stinchcomb, J.P. Regd. 5 Feb. 1802.

Elbert, Bk. H, 1802-1803:

p.1   Elbert Co., GA: 18 Sept. 1800, John Andrew & Mary O., his wife, to William O. Robins, all of sd. co., for $30, 6 acres, where he now lives. (signed) John Andrew, Mary O. Andrew. Wit: Hezekiah Gray, J.P. Regd. (torn off).

Oglethorpe, Bk. D, 1800-1806:

p. 373   Elbert Co., GA: 10 Aug. 1799, John Andrews &

Mary O., his wife, of Elbert Co., to James Jordan of Oglethorpe Co., for $90, 40 acres in Oglethorpe Co. on Long Creek, Dry Fork waters, adj. NE by Abram Hill, N. by Blake, SE by Jordan, beg. post oak, N12E24 30 ch. 75 links to Spanish oak, N70W 35 ch. to red oak, N12E 24 ch. 50 links to beg., orig. granted to John Andrews. (signed) John Andrews, Mary O. Andrews. Wit: A. Stinchcomb, J.P. Ack. 19 Oct. 1804, Francis M. Gilmer, Hezekiah Gray, J.P.

p. 497 24 Aug. 1801, Robert Duncan to John Bailey, both of Oglethorpe Co., for $1000, 200 a. on Whites Creek in said co., adj. S. by John Andrews, W. by Saml. Cochran, N. by Jesse Bolls, E. by John Cargile & James Daniel, was granted to Robert McCrary in Aug. 1784, in fee simple. (signed) Robert Duncan. Wit: Ben Baldwin, J.I.C., Nancy Baldwin. Recorded 30 July 1805.

Elbert, Bk. K, 1806-1808:

p. 28 Lincoln Co., GA: John Andew of Elbert Co., GA, sold to me by Sheriff Hughes of Lincoln Co., GA, have sold to Solomon Rountree & Hugh Taylor, 2 negroes, Carter & Silvey, for $500, 8 Apr. 1799. (signed) John Andrew. Wit: John Posey, R. McDougall. Chatham Co., GA: Bill of sale proved by Robert McDougall, 9 Aug. 1806, Saml. H. Stackhouse, old city Savannah. Regd. 25 Sept. 1806.

Elbert, Bk. O, 1812-1813:

p. 76 Elbert Co.: 13 Oct. 1802, John Andrew to Thomas B. Scott, 1 sorrel mare & colt, 5 cows & calves, 1 sow & 7 pigs, 5 beds & furniture, 3 pots & 2 ovens, 2 tables, 3 bedsteads, 1 dish, 30 volumes of books, for $250. (signed) John Andrew. Test: David Connally, Hezekiah Gray, J.P. Rec. 6 Oct. 1812.

p. 76   Rountree & Taylor vs. Andrew & Scott. Fifa. The firm of Rountree & Taylor, 10 May 1802, received from Thomas B. Scott, one of the defendants, amount in full of above execution. I as survivor of the firm, do relinquish to Thomas B. Scott, without liability to myself or to the late firm, the entire use & control of the execution, 29 Aug. 1812. (signed) Hugh Taylor. Rec. 6 Oct. 1812.

Elbert, Bk. P, 1813-1816:

p. 25   Elbert Co.: Sundry executions issued from Superior Court of sd. co. One in favor of Rountree & Taylor against Andrew & Scott, 19 Apr. 1802. The other in favor of Jesse White against John Andrew, 17 Oct. 1803. 26 Aug. 1812, James Wood, Shff. of sd. co. levied executions on a woman named Maria & a woman named Tamer & her 5 children, Nelson, Milsy, Synthia, Jefferson, & Louisia, a woman named Bess & her 3 children, Evelina, Sam, & Eady, a woman named Cloe & her 3 children, Milinda, Madison, & Billey, & 3 other women named Silvia, Milly, & Tenor. 1st Tues. in Oct. 1812 at the courthouse in sd. co., exposed to public sale the negroes in sundry lots & Thomas B. Scott, Esqr. of Putnam Co., GA was the highest bidder, for $3792, all claim John Andrew had in negroes at time of judgement, 6 Oct. 1812. (signed) James Wood, shff. Wit: Geo. Cook, Archelus Jarratt. Elbert Co.: bill of sale proved by Archelus Jarratt, 2 Feb. 1814, Richard Fortson, J.P. Rec. 10 Feb. 1814 Wm. Woods, clk.

p. 40   Elbert Co.: 24 May 1810, Thomas Goolsby of Randolph Co., GA to John L. Goolsby of Elbert Co., for $350, all tract said to be 150 a. on Falling Creek waters, lately sold to Thomas by Benjamin Goss, Senior, adj. Joshua Clark, Hezekiah Gray, Henry Kinnebrew & John Andrew, in fee simiple. (signed) Thomas Goolsby. Wit: J. McCoy, J.P., Jared Beasley, J.P. Rec. 22 Feb. 1814 Wm. Woods, clk.

p. 40   7 Dec. 1812, John Goolsby of Elbert Co., GA, to James Beveridge of Oglethrope Co., GA, for $275, tract where sd. John Goolsby now lives, sd. to be 150 acres in Elbert Co. on Falling Creek, adj. Joshua Clark, Hezekiah Gray, Henry Kinnebrew & John Andrew, in fee simple. (signed) John T. Goolsby. Wit: Andrew West, Reuben Goolsby, A. Jarratt. Elbert Co.: proved by A. Jarratt, 22 Feb. 1814, Robt. B. Christian, J.P. Rec. 22 Feb. 1814 Wm. Woods, clk.

p. 100   Elbert Co., GA: 10 Oct. 1814, William S. Spencer mortgage to Joseph Brawner, both of sd. co., for $175. Security is tract on Falling Creek waters formerly property of John Hubbard, late of the state of TN, decd., sold to me by heirs & attys. of Hubbard in sd. co. The tract adj. sd. Brawner on E., on which I now live said to be 148 acres on Cedar Creek waters, being part of tract surveyed by Sally S. Bibb & sold to Thomas Scott as guardian for James Andrew, minor. If warrantee deed made before 1 Jan. next to Brawner for the tract then this mortgage to be void. (signed) Wm. S. Spencer. Wit: John Andrew, J.N. Brown. Elbert Co.: mortgage proved by John Andrew who saw James N. Brown witness, 15 Dec. 1814, Henry Kinnebrew, J.P. Regd. 16 Dec. 1814 Wm. Woods, clk.

p. 102   Elbert Co.: 14 Mar. 1814, Thomas B. Scott of Putnam Co., GA, to James O. Andrew of Elbert Co., GA, for $500, all the tract sold to him by John Andrew in Liberty Co., GA, in formerly St. Johns Parish on headwaters of Newport & Midway Swamps, adj. the desert granted to John Winn, formerly the property of Lydia Winn, decd., adj. Rodger P. Saunders & Benjamin Andrews, said to be 300 acres. (signed) Thomas B. Scott. Wit: H. Gray, A. McGehee. Regd. 18 Dec. 1814.

Elbert, Book T, 1822-1824:

p. 122 Elbert Co.: 1 May 1802, John Andrew to Thomas B. Scott, both of sd. co., for $50, Lot No. 7 in the town of Elberton, sd. co., 1 acre, adj. Eli Eavenson, Woods & others. (signed) John Andrew. Wit: Wm. Cunningham, J.P. Rec. 17 Apr. 1824.

Comments on his Father
by James O. Andrew

The following quotations are abstracted from the volume, *The Life and Letters of James Osgood Andrew*, by George G. Smith, Southern Methodist Publishing House, Nashville, TN, 1883, pp. 15-37, 212-215. They detail Smith's account of the origin of this family as well as comments from Bishop J.O. Andrew on his father.

"In the days of Charles the First and his persecuting archbishop, John White, the grandfather of John Wesley was the pastor of a Puritan church in Dorchester, England. The times were stormy, and he resolved, with his church, to emigrate to Massachusetts, and secured a grant of lands. Not far away was the town of Plymouth, in which there was a sister church, which was to go with him and his. The church at Dorchester may not have emigrated; Dr. White certainly did not. The church at Plymouth did come to America, and established the town of Dorchester, Massachusetts. After fifty years this church set out a colony to South Carolina, and the town of Dorchester, South Carolina, was established on the Ashley River, fifteen miles from Charleston. The colonists and their descendants remained here for fifty years.

In the meantime Georgia was settled, and as they were cramped for lands, after due examination, and after having secured a large grant from the Georgia Colonial Government, they crossed the Savannah River and settled some fifty miles south of the city of the same name, at a place they called Midway, and where they founded another Dorchester.

Among these colonists were two Andrews, James and Benjamin. Benjamin is mentioned as having a family. Which of these two was the grandfather of James Osgood Andrew I cannot say; probably Benjamin.

The pastor of the church was Mr. Osgood. In a sketch of his parents by Bishop Andrew, published in the *Home Circle*, he speaks of Mr. Osgood as his uncle. I can find nowhere else any indication that this was so, and am satisfied that it was the mistake of the editor of the *Home Circle*, who was misled by the statement of Bishop Andrew that his father was brought up by his uncle and educated by Mr. Osgood. It is certain John Andrew was much attached to his old pastor, and named his son James in his honor.

The father of John Andrew was a very pious man. He had a regular family worship, and once a week read a sermon to his family. While the son was quite a small boy the father died, and he was brought up by his uncle and educated by Mr. Osgood. He says he was not inured to hard labor; much to his after regret. He had a very correct English education, and knew something of Latin.

The old Puritan blood was the first Georgia blood to boil when the fires of the Revolution began to blaze, and John Andrew, then not quite grown, began to ride with Screven. He was a partisan ranger during the war.

After the war ended he found his slaves gone and his other property much injured, and he went from Liberty County into the new purchase.

Five years before the Revolution began, Sir James Wright, then Governor of Georgia, purchased from the Indians, a most beautiful and fertile country north and west of Augusta, extending to the banks of the Oconee. A part of this country was called Columbia County, and into it John Andrew came to teach a school. It was, for the time, rather thickly settled with a fine class of settlers. He was either married when he came or he married soon after. He lost his first wife after the birth of her first child; married again, and when she too had one child she died.

Although he was a member of the church at Midway, and strictly moral, he does not seem to have been a converted man.

The Methodists came into this section when they came to Georgia, and were making quite a sensation in it. The pathetic Major and the fiery Humphries were sweeping through the country, preaching as they went. The usual phenomena which attend evangelical preaching when it is first given to a simple-hearted people attended their labors. The steady-going young Puritan heard of the noise and confusion of the meetings, and decided to go and see for himself. It is the same often-told story. He went to condemn them, and ended in condemning himself. He cried for pardon and joined in society.

It was not long before he was called for. No man could be a laggard in those days –the harvest was too great, the laborers were too few; and so, in 1789, John Andrew began to ride again, not with Screven this time, but with Reuben Ellis, on the Cherokee Circuit, in South Carolina. The next year he was in Burke County, Georgia, and then he was on the Washington Circuit, where he married a third time, and, of course, located.

Just after the Revolution a body of Virginians, induced by Colonel George Mathews, removed from their own State, and settled on the Broad River, in Wilkes County, Georgia. Among these settlers was a Mr. Cosby. He was from Spottsylvania County, and a man well-to-do in the world. He was, while in Virginia, an adherent, if not a communicant of, the Episcopal Church. John Major, Thomas Humphries, Richard Ivy, Hope Hull, had all preached in Wilkes, and had built up strong societies, and some of the best people of the county had adhered to them. Among these was the gentle Mary Cosby and her sister. They did not unite with the Methodists without opposition."

Note: See the letter from Daniel Grant to Polly Cosby in the section of this volume containing family letters. Grant was a Presbyterian Elder in a church in Virginia and moved to the Wilkes Co., GA, area from North Carolina. Because Methodist preachers were the only ones nearby, he soon became a Methodist and built Grant's Meeting House. His letter encouraged the Cosby girls to become Methodists.

"When John Andrew came on the circuit, a young man of thirty-two, he wooed her and won her, and they were married. Her father seems to have been living at this time, for John Andrew speaks of a visit from Mr. Cosby two years afterward. Location always followed marriage in the early days of Methodism. The first man in this section of the Church to break the rule was James O. Andrew himself, and that was nearly twenty-five years from this time. So John Andrew located. He did not intend to cease from preaching, nor did he do so, but he settled down to attend to secular affairs. Alas for him that he did.

He was then thirty-four years old. He was not strong in health, and by some means had lost all his property and was deeply in debt. Those were the days of imprisonment for debt, and he was in danger of the debtor's prison. He had left the home of his kindred, he had lost all his estate, had already, young as he was, lost two wives. He had married a lovely and devoted young woman who had left a home of affluence to share his lowly lot. They had a little farm and a few slaves, and he began to teach a country school. Teaching a country school and receiving six dollars per year of twelve full months for controlling rude boys and pleasing unreasonable parents, may be a means of grace to a man, by making him patient, but it is not calculated to make one's life brighter, and so John Andrew found it. He, however, gave himself to prayer, met Brother Crutchfield in band, rode out every Sunday and preached, and taught the negroes in Sunday-school. He met in class with the society, and his dark sky was often lit up by rays of heavenly light; but too often it was sadly clouded. He had trials enough at the best, and perhaps the early lessons he had learned among the Puritans at Midway, and the stress laid upon feelings in the early days of Methodism, led him to write bitter things against himself too frequently. So when he was sick and tired, and burdened, he groaned in the bitterness of his soul; but he never turned from the way.

The man who, passing through the valley of Baca, shall make it a well, or he who, passing through the valley of the shadow of death, fears no evil, may be happier, but he is not more blessed than he who says, 'Though he slay me yet will I trust in him.'

John Andrew's journal tells of more Decembers than Mays, and it tells the story of a sensitive, poor, heart-stricken man, smitten, as he felt, of God, and misjudged by men, plodding on in the way of duty. He kept a little journal in 1792, and from it I have gathered the foregoing facts.

He lived, immediately after his marriage, not far from Washington, and continued to live in the same neighborhood until the birth of his first son, in May of 1794. The journal reveals the straits to which he was even then reduced, but he was evidently at that time possessed of a home and of a few slaves, and was one of the leading teachers of the section. He was constantly engaged in his ministerial work on the Sabbath."

"Wilkes County was one of the best of the newly settled counties, and in it, May 3, 1794, James Osgood Andrew was born. The house, we may be sure, was a double-log cabin, and the surroundings very plain, but at this time quite comfortable.

The father was just thirty-six years old, and the mother perhaps ten years younger. Bishop Andrew had no memory of his birthplace, nor of the next home to which the family removed. This was in Elbert County, a county adjoining Wilkes on the north. The financial troubles of John Andrew, to which allusion has been made, seem to have been so far settled that he was enabled to embark his little property, with that of his wife, in merchandise. It was the often-told story in Methodist annals –failure and trouble. He lost his property, and he, always sensitive, feeling that he had lost his influence, and that he was censured by his brethren, withdrew from the society. He did not cease to pray in private nor in the family, nor did he cease to try to obey God. His exile from the Church does not seem to have been of a long duration, for he was evidently in the society in 1813. These disasters all came while James was a little boy, perhaps before he could remember.

His first memory was of the humble home, a father

burdened with care, and a mother toiling to help her husband along.

He was the oldest son; there were two daughters by the first marriages. In very early childhood he was quite delicate, but after the bankruptcy and the loss of all, he says he began to grow more hardy, made so by the very privations he was called upon to endure."

"John Andrew seems to have moved to Cedar Creek to merchandise, and James was sent to another teacher. He says, 'One morning my mother fixed me in a style a little better than usual, and my father took me up and carried me to an ancient house which stood on the edge of an old field, and handed me over to a rough-looking man whose face was covered with pock-pits, and, after a few moments, left me with this unlovely old man and a swarm of youngsters of various ages. This was the beginning of my school-boy life, I being at that time about five years old.'"

"The atmosphere of the humble home was eminently refining. Polly Cosby was a lady born and bred, and the best Puritan blood was in the veins of John Andrew – cavalier and Puritan united here. Though they were poor they were not mean, and James Andrew was brought up as high-toned a gentleman as Georgia had in it. The home was eminently a Christian home. The dear mother had given her young life to religion, and had with a great courage met all opposition and conquered it, and the faithful father had, amid all the storms, steered his course heaven-ward; but no hand but that of the grateful son should be peermitted to draw the portraits of the father and mother. He says: 'My father was apparently a stern man, and there were hours when he did not choose to converse, but at other times he was exceedingly communicative and pleasant. His countenance always afforded me a sure index of his frame of mind, and readily satisfied me as to whether I might approach him; and I was never slow to avail myself of the privileges which those hours afforded, for he was always at such times an instructive and delightful companion. To these delightful hours of intercourse I owe much, very much of whatever little improvement I may have subsequently made. In his discipline he was decided and inflexible. His laws were few and appropriate, but they were uniformly enforced. If I did wrong, violating any of those rules, he sometimes punished me by refusing to talk with me, and showing me always a look of displeasure. This was a painful and mortifying state of things, but he sometimes appealed to my feelings in a manner rather more direct. When he said to me, "I'll remember you for this offence," I only wished that he would apply the rod at once, instead of keeping me in suspense; for I well knew that, however long delayed, the punishment was certain. That was one of the promises he never failed to keep.

My father was a very religious man. Family worship was never neglected by him, and about once a week, at the hour for family worship, he gave his children a short but appropriate and solemn appeal on the subject of their religious interests. I remember well how these seasons used to impress me. In addition to this, he used often to take me with him at eventide to his place of secret prayer in the woods, and, leaving me some twenty yards behind him, kneel and wrestle earnestly with God. I often heard his groanings, and knew that much of that agony was on my account. Ah! I shall never forget those evening prayer scenes.

At length, after having battled with the storms of life till past his threescore and ten, the Master said, "It is enough; the warfare is ended; enter into rest." His affliction continued for some time, and through it all he continued patient and resigned, calmly and triumphantly resting on the God of his salvation. At his request I administered the holy sacrament to my dying father; and surely it was a season never to be forgotten. God's presence cheered us.

On the morning of the day on which he died, he called my weeping mother and said to her: "Don't be troubled about yourself and the children. God will provide for you; he has this morning promised me that he would." After this, having affectionately and solemnly charged us all to live so as to meet him above, he gently fell asleep in Jesus; and when we bore him to the neighboring churchyard and laid him in the quiet grave, I felt the words, "There the weary are at rest," applied to my mind very impressively. He had closed a tempestuous voyage, had reached the long-desired haven, and was at rest –sweet, hallowed, eternal. There I hope at last to unite with him and many other departed precious ones.

My mother, whose maiden name was Cosby, was a native of Spottsylvania County, Virginia; but whether she belonged to the first, or second, or third families, I do not know. But this I do know –she was lovely and good enough to have belonged to the first and highest of them all. While she was yet young her father removed to Georgia, and settled in that part of Wilkes which is now called Elbert County. Here my mother grew to womanhood, and here she became decidedly religious and attached herself to the Methodist Church –a step which at that time required considerable nerve, as Methodism was imperfectly understood and greatly persecuted. Her parents were Episcopalians, and were, of course, sternly opposed to her; yet, in the midst of all these hinderances, she boldly decided to follow her conscientious convictions and unite her fortunes with those of the people of her choice, which she did, and was probably among the earliest converts to Methodism in the State of Georgia. Her course subsequently was straightforward and consistent; a gentle, quiet spirit, never bold or confident in the expression of he religious feeling, yet uniformly religious, loving God and his Church, saying no harm of anybody, and doing all the good she could. My mother was no shouter, and I think at the time of my earliest recollections she was not very fond of shouting, though everything with her depended upon the character of the shouters. But she loved the house of God, and in the class-meetings and other means of grace she greatly delighted.

My father's misfortunes involved her in much trouble, bringing her into circumstances to which she was not accustomed. Poverty was upon her household, and she felt it was her duty to contribute, as far as possible, to the support and training of her children, not only by carefully husbanding the limited means placed at her disposal, but by contributing her own exertions to increase the store. She was a very industrious woman, and could ply her knitting-needles beyond almost any one I ever knew; and many a bushel of corn and many a piece of meat was contributed by her skill in this department to the sustenance of her household. This was certainly much better than to insinuate that her husband's bad management had brought the family into trouble.

I had as well say just here that my mother was a very great reader. I have seen her sit for hours absorbed in some interesting volume, while her fingers were rapidly doing their work with her knitting-needles. In the management of her children, she was kind and gentle, but firm and judicious, leading us by her kindness, but knowing well how to use the rod when it became necessary. I was the only son till I was grown, and of course I was in some danger of being a spoiled boy; and possibly, if my parents had continued in a state of prosperity, I might have been so, for I learned from my mother that I used to be very delicate. She was afraid of the rain and of the sunshine, and dreaded to have me endure the slightest exposure, lest it might give me a cold or a fever, and I was likely to grow up a poor, puny sprout; but it pleased God to send us poverty, and straightway the pail and puny boy had to go to the mill, often in the rain, and frequently in the cold, wintry days, without shoes. He had to become a boy of all work, which necessitated a good deal of exposure every day, and, as a consequence, he became tough, and healthy, and self-reliant. To this I am largely indebted for a good constitution, which has sustained a good many years of the wear and tear of itinerant life.

My mother took great pains to guide my young mind and heart in the ways of knowledge and peace. She taught my heart and my lips to pray before I can remember; so that I do not recollect a single day of my life in which I did not pray. She had read much, and was quite an intelligent woman, so that she was well qualified to guide my infant thoughts into the incipient paths of knowledge. She was passionately fond of poetry, and used often to convey to my mind many of those valuable maxims which have been largely influential in the formation of my character. I can now look back with lively interest to those precious moments when, with her boy standing beside her, she directed his childish heart to the character and religion of the blessed Saviour. And I remember how she used to lay he hands upon my head, and bless me. O! how often did she thus renew her dedication of me to God, and pray that he would make me a minister! and how she looked when, on one occasion, she said, "I would rather see you a faithful preacher of the gospel than emperor of the world!"

When I returned annually to visit my parents, we used to have quite a household jubilee; and my mother's kind heart devised all sorts of good things for her dear James, while my father smoked his pipe and blessed me, and my sisters were so happy because brother had come home. And when the time came for me to leave, O, how many blessings and prayers followed me to my next work! My precious mother's parting salute, as she threw her arms around my neck and kissed me, was, "And now, my son, remember that I live if you stand fast in the Lord, and continue faithful in the work of your Master."

As old age approached, she became more cheerful and happy, her confidence in God growing stronger as she neared the close of her journey. It was a prominent trait in her character that she thought kindly of everybody; hence, she never indulged in evil-speaking, and used gently to rebuke those who did so in her presence. She always put the best construction on the behavior of others, and where their conduct could not be justified, she yet hoped for the best, and was sure to bring in some mitigating circumstances. She was a charming specimen of a cheerful and happy old age, not growing sour with increasing years, but happier and more cheerful. The young people all loved and sought her company, and she delighted in having them about her, and in ministering to their enjoyment.

But at length the weary wheels of life stood still. She was attacked with a painful disease to which she had been some time subject. I was just closing a Conference at Athens, Georgia, when, hearing that she was ill, I hastened home in time to watch her closing hours, and receive her dying blessing. It was a sad thought that I could no longer look on my mother's venerable form, nor hear that voice which had been wont to instruct me and bless me so often. Still, it was a matter of devout thanksgiving to God that she had been spared to us so many years, that my children might know and love her, and that she might give them her dying blessing. I felt, too, that it was cause of gratitude to God that she had been so graciously sustained throughout her long and checkered pilgrimage, and that the grace of God was richly vouchsafed to her in her closing hours, so that she not only lived well, but died in the Lord. Thanks be to God for his unspeakable gift. My parents were not among the titled and the rich, but I glory in having descended from parents who loved, trusted, and served God, and whose faith finally triumphed over death, and showed them the way to the throne of God. There they rest, and there I hope to meet them.'"

* *

Words from a memorial sermon by Lovick Pierce: "I made the acquaintance of Bishop Andrew's family in 1809, in Elbert County, being Presiding Elder on the old Oconee District. The family was poor, but famous for the virtues of pure practical godliness. His father, the Rev. John Andrew, was a regular educator, teaching only an English school of a very respectable grade."

"Bishop Andrew's mother was one of nature's noble-women –ennobled by the charms of a pure, rational, fervent piety

–a woman of fine, practical, common sense, a mother whose speech was always with grace, seasoned with salt, that ministered grace to the hearer. Her maternal, domestic piety issued from her sanctified life like fragrance from a rose, until all that could inhale or absorb its nature became imbued with it. The beautiful imprint of all that was lovely in the moral and intellectual character of the mother was made upon her son."

* *

"His father's home was almost in a direct line from Athens to Madison, and as he lived in Athens and came to Madison every other Sabbath, he was able to make a weekly call at the old preacher's humble cabin. This was well, for the old soldier was near his end. He was now seventy-two years of age. As we have seen, he was a man of very poetic nature, somewhat moody, perhaps morbidly conscientious. He was one of those men, not rarely found, who do not fit exactly into any place – men who are never understood by those among whom they live. He had the sad faculty of failing in nearly everything he undertook except in living an upright Christian life. He had raised a large family, and they were all Christians. He was now near his rest, and this spring God gave him sleep.

Through God's good providence, the son was enabled to reach the dying bed of his dear old father, and he tells of it in his reminiscences. After the darkness of the night the day-gleam had burst on the good old man. John Andrew at last had found a world in which he was fitted to live.

The Bishop says: 'For several months past his cough rendered him unable to preach, and confined him mostly to the house. On my return from our last Conference I found him sinking very rapidly, but his soul was peaceful and happy. He told me that he had prayed that he might be permitted to see me once more, that his petition was granted, and now he was willing to depart. My duties called me away from him for a little more than

159

a week, and when I again visited him he was in the same happy state of mind, waiting patiently for the change. The morning subsequent to my arrival he was taken with a violent fit of coughing which we thought had finished the struggle, but after some time he revived, although he could not articulate distinctly for nearly half an hour. As I sat by him I discovered that he wanted to speak. I asked him if he wanted anything; he replied, "Nothing but Christ. When I have Jesus in my soul all is well." During the greater part of the day he was employed in exhortation and in shouting the priases of God. A few days previous to his death he asked me to give him the Sacrament. God so far enabled me to control my feelings as to comply with this dying request, and we had a memorable family Sacrament. My mother and most of the children knelt around, and we all together for the last time commemorated the precious love of God to our guilty race. It was a moment of glorious exultation to my dying father, and so the good old man passed away. He was buried near where he had lived, and twenty-five years afterward the gentle Mary, his faithful wife, was laid beside him, and there they sleep.'"

Article on the Journal
from the Wesleyan Christian Advocate

On 1-2-1908, George G. Smith wrote an article entitled, "John Andrew's Journal," that was published in the *Wesleyan Christian Advocate*. The portions of the journal he published in the article are so identified in the chronological journal listings on earlier pages. Some of Smith's commentary, not found elsewhere, is given below:

"The Journal exhibits a conscientious, earnest, sensitive man struggling against odds and given to deep depressions, but tells often the story of great religious peace.

A traveling showman brought a camel through the country and the children wanted to go and see it, but he seriously objected, and was greatly disturbed at the sinful curiosity which the parents gratified by letting them go.

A boy gathered some fruit on Sunday and he chastised him to the displeasing of his parents. He says of himself, 'I am in the thirty-fourth year of my age, five years spent in stupor, ten in recovering learning, two in merchandise, some time with a doctor, a while with a parson, some years a soldier, then a farmer; two times a school master, for 7 years past, a circuit preacher, 3 times a married man, twice a widower, then a farmer and at last a master.' By master he means that he was then a slave holder.

Mr. Cosby evidently gave his wife some negroes and though John Andrew on principle was opposed to slavery, he received them, and mentions with sorrow that he had to punish one by whipping. He thought, however, the demand of the church for emancipation or expulsion was unwise. He never returned to the itinerancy and for awhile was 'out of society,' but never lost his religious fervor, or consistency.

The county in which he lived was then a frontier county which had been settled by Virginians mainly. There were some of them wealthy for those days, and lived in great comfort. He mentions them freely and speaks of their various deficiencies. Bro. Crutchfield did now want his daughters taught to cipher, 'although he made a subscription to the Wesley and Whitfield College, which never opened.' Bro. Grant was much too absorbed in merchandise. Richard Ivey and Jonathan Jackson and Bro. Hollday were preachers. He speaks of meeting in band and knowing his soul blessed and of many a dark hour and heavy trials. He lived to see his son James a famous preacher and to be cared for by him, in his declining years. He came back into the society and died in it. It is probable that John Andrew, who was an elder in the Presbyterian Church at Welton, SC, was his great grandfather and that he came from the same people who settled Dorchester, MA, and that he was a kinsman of the Massachusetts War Governor, who bore the same name, John Andrew.

His wife, Mary Cosby Andrew, long survived him and when her son James was made Bishop, he built her a neat home near his own, at Chestnut Grove, and in my childhood I remember a visit my mother made to the cottage to spend a night when I was with her. Mrs. Andrew was then a lovely old matron, living with her maiden daughter and a crippled son who was a teacher. I have no history of the church at Dorchester, MA, and do not know whether there was any Andrews in that colony. The family there were Puritans and people of some culture. Bartram, the famous naturalist, stopped at Benjamin Andrew's house for some days in his famous botanical journey through the South and among the first of the patriots and a leading man among them was Benjamin Andrew, the uncle of John Andrew. I hope some New England antiquarian will look into the history of Dorchester, MA, and see if there was an Andrew family then. I cannot find Benjamin Andrew in Virginia or MD, until the Revolution, when Benjamin Andrew the second went to VA and served in the army there as a lieutenant.

John Andrew had three sons: James Osgood who became Bishop, Harbut who never married and William of whom I know nothing. Bishop Andrew left one son, Rev. James O. Andrew who died recently and of his grand-children, Rev. Dr. Lovett, Rev. James M. Lovett and Rev. Charles A. Rush, of Alabama are in the itinerancy. I think his negro Sunday-school in Elbert in 1792 was the first Sunday-school among the Methodists for negroes and ante-dates any for white children."

Smith concluded that the portion of the journal in his possession for the writing of this article began in 1792 and ended on the 16th of July. As to the actual document, he stated at the outset of the article, "...and in 1792, kept a little journal. A fragment of which lies before me."

Gilmer's Account

George Rockingham Gilmer, a member of one of the families who came with Governor Matthews to settle the Goosepond area of what became Oglethorpe County, Georgia, wrote a memoir in 1855 called, *First Settlers in Upper Georgia,* in which he enumerates and comments upon various families who moved there from Virginia. The following is taken from pp. 119-121:

"Mary Cosby, the sister of Mrs. William Harvie, married John Andrew, a Methodist preacher. He quit the circuit for his locality, which was on the Elbert side of Broad River, opposite to Mr. William Harvie's, where he commenced the trade of merchandise with the property which he got with his wife, and the very little which he had himself. The spirit of trade and the spirit of preaching never agree together. One or the other will get the upper hand, if the unnatural union is continued. It is certain that John Andrew failed in trade, and found many stumbling blocks in the way of preaching. After all his property was taken to pay his mercantile liabilities, and he and his wife left to labor without assistance for their own and their children's support, he took to school keeping. The little ones are pretty sure to have a sore time who learn their ABCs from a harrassed, broken trader. Many had knowledge forced upon them by the switching looks of John Andrew. Being very hard visaged, he appeared as if he was always ready to cut the truant scholar in two. The pay for school keeping was in early times, in upper Georgia, the poorest pittance. The people wanted their children for work and kept them at it, except at leisure times, and when schooling could be had cheap. John Andrew, his wife and children, had to scuffle and pinch to provide food, and often-times, with all their exertions, found it scarce. It was then that the spirit of devotion strengthed the spirit of the wife and mother in her cares, and comforted her in her troubles.

Mrs. Andrew had loved her husband, homely as he was, with increased affection, because of the holy purposes of his life. It is in sore trials and great suffering that woman's love shows its true value. Mrs. Andrew made herself more precious than gold when her husband's purse became empty. With the strong faith of a true Christian, she labored without ceasing during her life, to perform all the duties of wife and mother. The blessing of heaven never fails to follow the prayers and industry of such a wife and mother. Her oldest son James, excited by her spirit and example, worked hard in the field during the day, collected light-wood knots on his return home, and toiled by their light after knowledge during the night. Nobody works in vain who works aright. The light which enlightens the world shined into the heart of James Andrew so brightly, that he could not restrain his desire to be the medium of communicating it to others. He was licensed to preach. The brotherhood by whom the license was granted, when they heard his first sermon regretted what they had done, so hesitating and unsatisfactory was the young enthusiast's efforts. But the right spirit was in him, though the knowledge and aptness to communicate had not been acquired. James Andrew found the assistance, which in his devotion he asked for, to aid his efforts to overcome the deficiencies of ignorance and inexperience. He soon made himself greatly superior in learning and the art of public speaking to those who were most opposed to his being licensed. And now the Methodist Church has no member of greater usefulness, nor one more efficiently devoted to the great purpose of its organization –the making known, with power in simplicity, the truths of the Gospel – than Bishop Andrew.

Herbert Andrew, the second son of Mrs. Andrew, had his dependence as a child increased by disease, which made him a cripple for life: His feet and legs became so contracted as to rest on his body instead of the ground. When other children were running about, he was confined to his mother's side. Whilst thus seated, receiving her instruction how to read, he heard from that fond, devoted, pious mother, how the best and holiest of all had suffered without repining, because it was the will of his Heavenly Father, until there came upon the spirit of the deformed boy the strongest desire to imitate his example. Herbert Andrew struggled to do whatever was possible in aid of his mother, in her hard effort to support her family, and effected more than most imagined possible. When he had learned what his mother could teach him, he went to school, moving upon his hands instead of his feet. By his mother's assistance, some little schooling, and his own untiring exertions, he qualified himself for teaching others. He has not been teaching near twenty years. His energy and ceaseless industry have secured him the greatest success. Whilst keeping school, he has acquired by his unassisted exertions such knowledge of the various departments of learning, that his scholars are admirably qualified for entrance into college. His pure life, the strength of his determination in overcoming difficulties, and the energy of his efforts in doing good, made such an impression upon the people among whom he lived, that they gave him some assistance by electing him to a public office, the duties of which he could discharge without intefering with the attention due to his school.

Mrs. Andrew's burdens were increased by her care for her husband's deaf, blind, dumb brother, whose filthy habits and irascible disposition added to the unbearableness of his idiocy. He put him into a hut in the yard of the family cabin. Every morning the unfortunate came out by light, walked round the hut twenty times; then went to each of three trees close by, and round them twenty times; then to the cabin-door, stepped on the sill with his left foot foremost, and down twenty times; then with his right foot foremost, and down twenty times; then went into the cabin, put his hand on the facing of the door and thumped the upper part twenty times; then thumped below twenty times; and then ate voraciously of what was prepared for breakfast. This unvaried round was continued for near twenty years, and until his death. When the idiot became outrageous, as he often did, Mrs. Andrew would lay her hand upon his arm. It quieted him, as if he felt the force of sympathy coming from her kind heart. He regarded nobody else. Cut off from society by constant confinement at home – seeing there at all times the most painful object which is ever looked upon – her children harrassed – the scanty food and clothing which she provided for them by her own hard labor, divided with one who had no good quality, and without hope, and incapable of being made better – Mrs. Andrew never forgot to care for the idiot, and to do for him all possible good – thus giving to the world an example of love and charity, which the world for its own sake should keep in perpetual remembrance."

Elsewhere in his memoir, Gilmer mentions some of the relations and neighbors of the Andrews. Remembering that the sister of Mary Cosby married William Harvie, the following excerpts shed light upon the Harvie and Cosby families:

"William Harvie was social, kind-tempered, well read, and conversable. His schemes were not always very practical, but were sustained with never-failing plausibility. His federal politics excluded him from holding office, except that of the Inferior Court, which having to pay attached to it, and yet requiring intelligence and integrity for the property discharge of its duties, was filled by the patriotic, whose services could be obtained without any investigation about their opinions of Jay's treaty or the French Revolution. He married Judith Cosby, the sister of the celebrated Judge Cosby, of Kentucky, and of James Cosby of Elbert County, Georgia, gentlemen of great worth and intelligence. Mrs. Harvie was a most amiable woman. Her pure and blameless life left an impression upon her children which may yet be seen in their intercourse with the world. Mr. & Mrs. Harvie joined the Methodist Church during the great revival of religion among the Broad River people in 1809, and gave ample evidence through their after lives of their sincere piety.

William Harvie had no son. His daughter Lucy was his darling pet child, who read to him, and talked to him of what she read. He loved flowers, and cultivated them successfully when all others on Broad River, considered such labor lost. A rose bush in one corner, and a hollyhock in another, was about as much as was allowed room for in the Broad River gardens of the things which could not be eaten. There is no training of the affections in the social state like the impressions made upon a daughter by the devoted love and care of a fond father. William Harvie's daughter Lucy continues to love and cultivate flowers, as if the pleasure derived from their fragrance and beauty is increased by the knowledge of the enjoyment which her father derived from the same sources. Lucy Harvie married Asbury Hull, whom every body has trusted from his youth with increasing confidence. They have six sons. Their oldest are men of genius and of the greatest social worth; their younger sons promise to equal in merit their older brothers..

William Harvie's daughter Martha married West Harris, a Methodist preacher. His daughter Genette married Mr. Van Lenard, a gentleman of fortune and respectability. His daughter Margaret married Mr. Littlebury Watts, who has been a member of the Legislature, and received other evidences of the confidence of his fellow-citizens. His youngest daughter, Mary, married John T. Groves, a graduate of Franklin College, who has devoted his life to the useful employment of educating the youth of his country."

William Harvie's brother, Richard, and his family are also enumerated in Gilmer's account. Richard's child, Margaret, married into a family touched upon in John Andrew's journal:

"Margaret Harvie married John Devenport, who belonged to a numerous family, most of whom were in the habit of fuddling their very good intellects by drinking whiskey. John was, to his credit, a sober, industrious man, who made a good estate. His chief merit was to be found in his success in marrying a wife of the most admirable qualities."

John Andrew, Patriot

In 1969, Fred P. Davenport, then Superintendent of Schools in Wyandotte, Michigan, wrote a booklet entitled, "John Andrew, Patriot." Davenport attempted to give an accurate historical account of Andrew's life and lineage. The following are excerpts from his 13 page work:

"John Andrew was born September 14, 1758, in Midway Colony, St. John's Parish, Georgia of a prominent family. His father, James Andrew, was a prosperous landowner. His uncle, Benjamin Andrew, was one of the big figures in the public life of Georgia from about 1760 until several years after the Revolution, holding almost every appointment within the gift of the Province and State except that of Governor.

Following his father's death in 1770, John lived with his uncle by marriage, Reverend John Osgood, minister of the Midway Church, until his death in 1773.

James Andrew, John's father, practically decreed in his will that John be trained for the ministry. 'My will,' he wrote, 'is my children shall have proper education, and my eldest son (John) shall be kept at school until he has learned the Latin tongue, and then if his tutors and the minister for the time being shall be of the opinion he has a capacity to be useful, and his disposition encouraging, and the income of his porportion of my estate will admit of it, he may have what further education is requisite if to be obtained with conveniency.'"

"John enlisted July 24, 1776, in the 3rd South Carolina Regiment commanded by Colonel William Thompson. He subsequently served under or with Wade Hampton, Henry Hampton, General Elbert, General Screven and General Sumter as private, ensign, adjutant and quartermaster. There are records which show, further, that a John Andrew served under Marion.

This patriot was exceedingly proud of his service. Many years later John observed about himself as 'yet I no traitor's dress have worn.' In a letter dated July 14, 1856, one of his sons, Reverend James Osgood Andrew, commented as follows:

'I will give you as far as I recollect . . . the information which I ... have often heard from his own lips as to his soldier's experience. My father was born and raised in Liberty County, Georgia. When the war broke out and its calamities were felt in Georgia, he in common with many others left home. He belonged to what was known as the Georgia Refugees. He served sometime in South Carolina under Sumter (and) was, I think, part of the time in the regiment of Col. Hampton, and I have heard him speak of his acting as Quartermaster. How long he acted in this capacity I do not know but I remember to have heard him speak of the fact several times as he would sit and tell us of his war-like exploits and hairbreadth escapes. He was with Sumter at the time of his defeat and has often given me the history of that unfortunate engagement. He was also at the Battle of Briar Creek in Georgia and so accurate were his descriptions of the ground and events of that engagement that I remember to have heard Chas. H. Sanders of Covington say that when a few years since he visited the spot he recognized the spot distinctly from my father's description of it. He was also with Col. Clarke at Augusta. Of these matters I have a distinct recollection because his recital of them used to afford me so much pleasure in my boyish days, and my father was like other old soldiers who love to fight their battles o'er.'

This old soldier was granted 287 & ½ acres of land in Washington County on December 13, 1785, for his military service. He drew 202 & ½ acres of land in Coweta County as a Revolutionary soldier in the Land Lottery of 1827.

John took Ann Lambright as his bride on February 10, 1779. They were wed at the Ervahns, South Carolina, by a Reverend Gourley. Eleven months and ten days later their daughter, Ann, was born. Shortly afterwards mother Ann died.

Just what John did during the next few years is not completely clear. It is known that he tried his hand at merchandising briefly and without success. It also is known that he served at least two terms in the Georgia House of Assembly, for the minutes dated January 13, 1783, read in part: 'John Andrew, returned a member from Liberty County, took the oath.'

As his second wife John chose his cousin, Mary Buer Andrew, one of Benjamin's daughters. (Another of Benjamin's daughters married Colonel Henry Hampton; thus John became a brother-in-law of sorts to his former commanding officer). John and Mary were married September 20, 1785 at Colonel's Island by the Reverend Abiel Holmes, father of Oliver Wendell Holmes. Mary had one daughter, also named Mary Buer, before here death in 1786.

John accompanied his father-in-law and uncle, Benjamin, to Augusta around 1787. It was here that he turned to teaching, a calling which he was to follow, except for two brief interludes, until his death.

In 1790 when the Methodist Conference was held at Grant's Meeting House in Wilkes County, which was the first Methodist Church in the State, (**Note:** untrue), Methodism was in its infancy. It was here that John Andrew, who had only recently been converted and was preaching in South Carolina, entered the Conference. In doing so he joined the ten other ministers –this was the total for the Conference – and became the first native of Georgia admitted into the traveling ministry. He knew bishops Asbury and Coke, and was closely associated with such religious pioneers as Daniel Grant, David Meriwether, Isaac Smith, Hardy Harbert and Hope Hull. He is in a very real sense one of Methodism's historic figures.

John Andrew's circuit included the Broad River Colony. One of its leading settlers was Charles Cosby who had removed himself to Georgia from Spottsylvania County, Virginia. It was one of his daughters, the gentle and genteel Mary Overton who was known to her friends as Polly, that John wooed and won as his third wife. Following their wedding on December 11, 1791, John located. Once again he turned to teaching. He continued to teach and to preach until March 10, 1830, when he departed from this life."

"John and Polly Andrew had ten children, seven of whom reached adulthood. All were upright, contributing citizens, their youngest, Hardy Harbert, was an outstanding student at Emory University and won renown as an exceptional teacher. This was accomplished in spite of the handicap of a warped spine. Beyond any question Hardy Harbert became what he was in large part because of his parents.

Their oldest, James Osgood, became a Bishop in the Methodist Church. He was the outstanding minister of his day, and it was over him that the Southern faction of Methodism was formed in 1844. Histories have been written about this man. In evaluating him, Alexander H. Stephens, vice-president of the Confederacy, stated, 'No man stands higher.' Beyond any question James Osgood Andrew became what he was in large part because of his parents.

A daughter of John and Polly, Elizabeth, died in 'perfect peace.' She was a devout Methodist, a person of exceeding kindness and the mother of thirteen children. Of her seven sons, three were killed and three were wounded in the Civil War. The seventh was a physician who served both soldiers and civilians well. Beyond any question these children became what they were as adults in large part because of their parents. These, in turn, have been molded previously by their own parents.

Still another illustration is presented to underscore the wholesomeness of this man. While John is not mentioned specifically in this serendipity, it is only because he died before its author was many years of age. His influence unquestionably helped create the atmosphere so delightfully described by his granddaughter, Henrietta Andrew Meriwether, when writing to her aunt.

My Dear Aunt:

I have been reading Pa's account of his parents in the last Home Circle and it has opened the flood gates of memory, and brought such a rush of old scenes before me that I felt like I wanted to talk to you about it.

When he speaks of his coming home to see his mother and the family, and how all tried to make his visits pleasant, and add in every possible way to his happiness, how distinctly came before my mind the old place in Clark, and I seemed to see again my dear precious grandmother as she looked so pleased to have us with her, and when our boisterous gayety would bring a reproof from ma, how sweetly she would say, 'Do Amelia, let the poor things play.'

And there, too, is the little trundle bed where dear Uncle Harbert used to sit, that was our first aim when we came in. And, Oh! how we used to frolic, and I, poor pepper pod, would get hurt, and then mad, but in five minutes I was at it again as bad as ever.

I do not think such a man as Uncle H. ever existed, I was going to say, but I will say I never saw such an one with all his afflictions –and his Maker alone knows how great they were – so cheeerful, with such an unfailing flow of spirits, and such a happy faculty of making himself beloved by young people.

I remember, too, going with him to the school house (you remember where it stood) and the spring, and the nice little gourd that hung on a bush over it for the boys and girls to use.

There is another thing I know you remember and that is the old spring house. Don't you see now how we used all to look going down the hill, you with the pitcher and spoon, Sallie with the butter milk pitcher, and I with the butter plate. That was a glorious old spring, and I thought that surely the spring house, and branch, and all the surroundings made it the most delightful spot I ever saw. It still seems so to me.

There is another thing I know you remember, how Sallie

and I used to go with you and Aunt Caroline to the cow pen. We bothered you too much for you ever to forget it. We used to jump on the calves backs and ride through the field, tearing through briars and bushes, and the end of it was that the dresses were so torn that we were afraid to let ma see how rude we had been, and then how kindly one or the other of you would mend it and say nothing about it.

And Aunt Lucy, too, was there with her brighteyed baby that we used to admire as a perfect beauty, and beautiful he was, too.

Uncle Will, too, came in for his share of botheration with us. There was always something or other we were calling upon him for, and grandma would say, 'Now William child, do whatever it is the poor things want you to do.' I tell you, the sun never shone upon a more genial soul than that beating in grandma's bosom. She knew we were cooped up in town all the time and she intended we should enjoy our visits up the country to the full, and indeed we did.

I haven't forgotten our fishing frolics either, but we always had to look to Aunt Caroline for that. If you went with us you were thinking about so many other things to be done at home that you could not stay long. And when Pa went—whew—we might as well have stayed at home, for he would decide in a few minutes that there was no fish in the creek, and if they were there we would never catch them, and so back home we would go unless when Aunt C. came to the rescue and stayed with us as long as we pleased. I have often throught surely no children ever had such indulgent aunts as we did, and I have never forgotten their kindness and never shall.

But what a letter I have written. Well, I can't help it if it is out of the ordinary one. All my excuse is I felt like writing it.

Do give a good deal of love to all the kin folks for us. We should have been out there this winter if I had been able to go, but I have been too unwell all winter to leave home. I haven't written half I wanted but I won't tire you out, so goodbye. Mother

M M and Jim all join in love. How I wish you would come and make us a visit: Goodbye.

Yours most affectionately,

Hennie'

Mr. Davenport cited many footnotes for the above facts. Some of his sources, not mentioned elsewhere, are listed here for identification: *The Georgia Genealogical Magazine,* n12 (April, 1964), p. 747, contains will of Lydia Winn, sister to Mary, wife of Rev. John Osgood; Rev. War Pension Claim W. 5623 file, National Archives, Washington, DC, containing letters written by relatives of John Andrew and by government officials verifying his service; Alexander Gregg, *History of the Old Cheraws,* p.405, identifies Andrew serving as adj. of Col. Hicks' Reg. from Feb-Nov, 1780; Eliza Bowen, *Story of Wilkes County,* pp. 129-30; a letter by William Davenport to L.J. Gartrell, 1-2-1864, in National Archives identifying Andrew's daughter, Elizabeth & her lineage. (Davenport was John Andrew's son-in-law).

In his preface, Davenport quoted an article from the *Wesleyan Christian Advocate,* written on 2-1-1906 by B.H. Mobley, citing the grave of John Andrew: "On the road leading from Bishop to Farmington in a clump of trees – oaks and cedar – is a large heap of stones, built up with corners square, about three feet high, four feet broad and seven feet long. We are told this is the grave of Rev. John Andrew, who was the father of Bishop Andrew. On either side of this are other graves, one of which is that of his wife—the gentle Mary Cosby—which is hers I do not know because they are unmarked. Near these graves once stood a Methodist Church –Mt. Zion. A heap of stones mark the site of the chimney.
Rev. G.G. Smith in his life of Bishop Andrew speaks of John Andrew moving from Elbert to Clark County, to Mt. Zion, a little hamlet about four miles north of Watkinsville. It may be there was a little hamlet by the name of Mt. Zion, but this grave and the site of this

176

church is about five miles south of Watkinsville in what is now Oconee, but formerly Clark County.

John Andrew was the father of Bishop Andrew, and is thus intimately associated with the very existence of the M.E. Church, South, for it was because the Northern wing sought to eject Bishop Andrew from the episcopacy, because of his connection with slavery through his wife, that the Southern wing seceded and organized the M.E. Church, South. He is also the grandfather of Dr. Lovett, one of the editors of the *Wesleyan*. So the name of John Andrew is connected with the historic past and the living present.

But the grave is unmarked, save by the heap of stones that in the course of time will fall to pieces. It seems that the great Southern Methodist Church ought to mark in some suitable way this neglected grave."

Author Fred Davenport was a descendant of Elizabeth Sydnor Andrew and William Davenport. His father was Frederick Davenport, son of Parks E. Davenport. Parks was the son of Overton Davenport who was a child of William Davenport and Elizabeth S. Andrew. Fred Davenport was reared in Eastland, TX and visited GA in 1966 to conduct research on the Andrew line.

177

The Grave of John Andrew

The grave of John Andrew is in a grove of oaks on the west side of U.S. 441 between Bishop and Farmington at the orange gate leading to the home of Johnny Michael. Michael bought the land from Daniel Branch.

A second marked grave in the cemetery is that of Malinda V. Akridge (11-20-1849 – 3-20-1855). She was the daughter of Virgil W. Akridge and wife who are also there. The dates on Virgil Akridge's grave are (11-5-1805 – 7-28-1849).

There are 10 oaks in one group near the highway and another large oak further back on a hill. That oak is near a foundational pillar, probably that of old Mt. Zion Church, that is propped against one of the 10 oaks. The graves are not visible from the highway due to boxwood hedges growing around them. One has to part the hedges to see the stone on the grave of Andrew.

This was undoubtedly a center-point of the Mt. Zion community of early times. In the 1950s, the farm containing these graves belonged to Otho M. Branch, Sr. Mr. Branch was born in 1883 and died in 1971. He is buried in the Farmington Community Cemetery across from the Methodist Church there. The church is the relocated Mt. Zion congregation that began on the Branch/Michael property.

Memoir of
The Rev. Hardy H. Andrew
by Bishop Andrew

The Rev. Hardy Harbert Andrew was born in Elbert co., GA, — I think, in 1813. While he was an infant, it was supposed that his nurse let him fall, and injured his spine, so that he was never able to walk; yet he was in all other respects a healthy child. To remedy this injury, my parents availed themselves of the best medical advice which their circumstances enabled them to command. All, however, was of no avail, and my brother grew up a cripple: he was never, I think, able to walk erect, but used to hop about with the aid of a block in each hand, his knees being drawn up in an unnatural and very uncomfortable position. Notwithstanding this he was exceedingly sprightly and cheerful in his disposition – was fond of books and learned very rapidly. This fondness for reading continued with him through life, and largely contributed to his own comfort and the happiness of those around him.

After the death of our father, Hardy was looked upon as the head of the household, and nobly did he sustain that relation till God called him home. He became a christian in early life, the precise date of his conversion I am not prepared to furnish, nor is it material: it is of much greater importance to know that his life was ever after one of consistent piety. He loved to talk of religion, and richly enjoyed its comforts: he loved the house of God, and delighted greatly in all the means of grace. He was a faithful and useful class leader, was very diligent in the work of Sunday Schools and in the promotion of the Temperance cause. For several years prior to his death he officiated as a local preacher and graduated to the office of deacon. As a preacher, he was, I understand, highly acceptable. God had endowed him a large measure of energy and independence: perhaps the world has presented but few instances of more indomitable energy and earnestness of purpose and effort. Thousands in his circumstances would have been crushed into absolute despondency, and excused themselves from any personal efforts, and felt themselves amply justified in looking to others for support. Not so, however, my beloved brother. Surrounded as he was by circumstances of appaling difficulty, having to grapple with poverty and with a disease which left him no hope of ever behing able to use his limbs, yet he knew no fear: he resolved to be independent, and to contribute to the aid of his fond widowed mother. This purpose he carried out bravely.

By dint of application to study, he qualified himself to teach: in this vocation he continued till God removed him from the earth, and his success was what might have been expected from his talent and faithfulness. Perhaps no man ever taught in Newton county who had acquired so extensive a reputation as a teacher – not merely as an English teacher – by dint of application he had prepared himself to teach the classics, and not a few of his pupils have entered Emory College, and graduated with credit to both their alma mata and to him who had directed their elementary studies.

For several years consecutively he was Tax collector for the county of Newton, and discharged the duties of his trust with ability and fidelity. His health had been for several years declining: he became subject to repeated attacks of rheumatism, and his sedentary life prevented the proper action of his bowels, so that he suffered greatly from colic; about eighteen months before he died he had a severe attack of rheumatism which deprived him of the use of his right hand. His friends then urged him to discontinue his school and live among them, assuring him of a home and a hearty welcome for the rest of his life, but the high-souled man refused: no, said he, I can yet do something; and he persisted in teaching a large school of nearly fifty scholars, though the scholars had to haul him in a little wagon to and from the school-house, and lift him into his seat when he got there.

In autumn of last year, he determined to accept the invitation of the Trustees of Emory College and take charge of the preparatory school at Oxford. He commenced his work, and was fast building up a school of high order, when worn out by disease and labor, the weary wheels of life stood still, and God called him to that rest for which he had long been toiling. The battle of life had been to him a stern and ragged one, but he had fought it bravely. And as I looked upon the poor emaciated body of my brother, I thought how sweet must the rest of heaven be to you after all your battling with the storms of life. He closed his pilgrimage about the first of June 1st. There was nothing remarkable in his last hours; they were calm and peaceful. I have extended this notice further than I intended, but it is the notice of no ordinary man. One who gave to the world conclusive proof that he was an honest, earnest, indomitable, God-fearing man; and I have thought that it might not be out of place to hold up to view the character of one who so nobly demonstrated how much can be done by one who fears God, trusts him, and with self-reliant energy throws himself upon the tide of life, to buffet its waves and do his duty.

Southern Christian Advocate
10-27-1854, p. 81.

www.ingramcontent.com/pod-product-compliance
Lightning Source LLC
Chambersburg PA
CBHW070917270326
41927CB00011B/2610